MW00411987

The Patriarch

The Patriarch

Essays from the Middle

Joshua Rice

RESOURCE *Publications* · Eugene, Oregon

THE PATRIARCH
Essays from the Middle

Copyright © 2023 Joshua Rice. All rights reserved. Except for brief quotations in critical publications or reviews, no part of this book may be reproduced in any manner without prior written permission from the publisher. Write: Permissions, Wipf and Stock Publishers, 199 W. 8th Ave., Suite 3, Eugene, OR 97401.

Resource Publications
An Imprint of Wipf and Stock Publishers
199 W. 8th Ave., Suite 3
Eugene, OR 97401

www.wipfandstock.com

PAPERBACK ISBN: 978-1-6667-7353-8
HARDCOVER ISBN: 978-1-6667-7354-5
EBOOK ISBN: 978-1-6667-7355-2

VERSION NUMBER 08/31/23

Scriptures taken from the Holy Bible, New International Version®, NIV®. Copyright © 1973, 1978, 1984, 2011 by Biblica, Inc.™ Used by permission of Zondervan. All rights reserved worldwide. www.zondervan.com The "NIV" and "New International Version" are trademarks registered in the United States Patent and Trademark Office by Biblica, Inc.™

To Gene Rice, our Patriarch.

"In those days there were giants in the land . . ."
—Genesis 6:4

Contents

Preface

How to Read
this Book

THAT IS A RATHER bold and annoying caption, as if presuming that you will struggle. The reality is more complicated than your reading skills, because it is my reality that you are entering.

This book is first and foremost a memoir, an exposé of moving from young adulthood into middle age while running many miles on the ground. However, I also happen to be a Bible scholar, on some days a pastor and on most days a Christian. I have so lived in the world of the biblical text since I was a child that it provides the involuntary game rules for how I interpret life, the world, winning and losing. I don't think about the Bible in a mechanical fundamentalist sense, though I do believe it holds many practical answers for human flourishing. For me, the Bible makes sense of the world and our shared human plight in the complexity of its narratives, which are often dark and twisted. God is the hero of the narratives, which can make for a lot of strangeness.

I have chosen the narratives about Abraham to try to make sense of this middle stage of life. I was drawn to him not primarily due to his historical significance—he is a towering figure in three major world faiths—but because he was a man who never seemed to arrive. He was always in between . . . spaces, relationships, and most of all, in between the divine promise and its fulfillment.

Though I have consulted and cite an array of scholarly sources on these ancient texts, especially rabbinic sources indicating how Jewish readers have understood their patriarchal forebearer over the millennia, this is not an academic book. It is more of a writing experiment. I have produced technical work on the Bible elsewhere. I am indeed often guided by scholarship and ancient readers, but I also make my own leaps. There may even be some ill-fated attempts at humor. In this sense, what I am doing with the Abraham story is similar to the ancient Jewish interpretive tradition called *Midrash*, or creative reading, where whosoever will is invited to jump into the fun. The Talmud says, "As a hammer divideth fire into many sparks, so one verse of Scripture has many meanings and many explanations."

Yet this is also not a Bible study per se, so my suggestion here is going to seem odd: it might make your experience easier if you have the book of Genesis nearby. I cite a portion of the passage that I am using at the top of each chapter, but it is typically just a snippet. If you aren't familiar with the Abrahamic narratives, it will not at all be burdensome to read them along the way. Bored you shall not be.

In summary, you are in for a memoir that includes a thousand miles of running and thousands-year-old texts. Now, let's hit the trail.

Glossary

Abram/Abraham—He is considered the father of the Israeli people; the first Jew. His original name, Abram, meant "father." Along the course of the biblical story, God changes his name to Abraham, which meant "father of many." This book stays true to the name that is used in each particular Genesis passage.

Hebrew Bible—Christian readers may be unaccustomed to this term in place of the "Old Testament," but each designates the same 39 books (though the sequence of books is different in each). Jewish readers also call this the Tanakh, from the first letter of three Hebrew words that respectively stand for Torah, the Prophets and the Writings.

Midrash—From the Hebrew root word meaning "to investigate" and "to interpret," these creative readings of biblical texts form the predecessors of Christian sermons. Often embellished with wild and vivid details and wholesale changes, they made the texts relevant to contemporary audiences. With regard to this book's subject, the custom of midrash "began to create a series of new-and-improved Abrahams."[1]

---

1. Feiler, *Abraham: A Journey to the Heart of Three Faiths*, 122.

Mishnah—From the Hebrew word meaning "to repeat," Jacob Neusner identifies this collection of sayings as "the first document of Rabbinic Judaism."[2] Compiled around 200 CE, it contains thousands of sayings of Jewish rabbis and sages from the first and second centuries, typically focused on Torah texts such as the Abraham narratives.

Rabbis—From the Hebrew word meaning "chief" or "master," rabbi is a term that began being used in the first century CE to refer to prominent Jewish sages and teachers. The rabbis were the progenitors of the Talmud and the Mishnah, the experts on interpreting the Torah texts.[3]

Talmud—From the Hebrew word, "learning," the Talmud is structured as thousands more sayings of the rabbis that comment on the Mishnah. It has been said that if Jews truly are a "people of the book," the book in question is the Talmud. "Be heedful in *Talmud*," one rabbi says, "for an unwitting error in *Talmud* is accounted a willful transgression."

Torah—From the Hebrew word, "law," these are the first five books in the Hebrew Bible (Genesis—Deuteronomy). They are often called the "Books of Moses" based on the traditional view of authorship and thus are especially sacred in Jewish tradition.

2. Neusner, *The Mishnah: A New Translation*, ix.

3. "Rabbinic literature often strikes the Western Christian reader as strange, a perception which has contributed to anti-Semitism. It is a closed, self-referential, elliptical body of literature which is understood only by those fully familiar with it." Saldarini, "Rabbinic Literature and the NT," 603.

Introduction

I WENT RUNNING IN midday last week, at a time in which I never run because the heat here in the deep south will fry eggs on the open road. Running is my salve and my lectern, the hour where I explore the limits of body and soul. I was pacing down Ebenezer Street, thinking about my father.

I am coming near the little elementary school, and I know this not because I am looking up, but because of the particular cracks in the road, splaying like webs. I know this road better than I know my own mind; looking up is optional. For whatever reason, I look up, and there he is, brown coat, jeans. He is twenty feet away, looking at the ground. I run past him, and he looks up at me, knowingly, half-grinning. His beard, his coat, his hair, his jeans, all a perfect match. My dad. I turn and look at his back after I pass, to see if he is actually there. He does not turn around.

A while later, I went to traffic court in the country. It was oddly melodramatic. The prosecutor led me to the dais over a routine speeding ticket. I looked up and the judge was my mother. She looked at me, knowingly, and assigned the fine. I paid it.

The evolutionary biologist J.B.S. Haldane wrote: "My own suspicion is that the Universe is not only queerer than we suppose, but queerer than we can suppose."[4]

4. Haldane, *Possible Worlds and Other Essays*, 298.

That was the day I realized it was time to heat the smelter and polish the anvil. That was the day I knew that this book was on its way. These odd sorts of things start to happen after you turn forty.

The coming of age saga is, I suppose, as old as literature, as old as thought. It is enshrined in Salinger (of course), Joyce, Lee, Dostoevsky, Dickens, Fitzgerald. It is etched into the biographies of ancient Rome and the epic poems of Homer. It is the tragic foundation of the Bible's creation story. Twenty years ago, I lived so many of these stories.

But now I am trying to figure out another story. I am trying to figure out what it means to not be young anymore, the second half. I am trying to figure out what to do with satisfaction, with boredom, with conquests that I wrestled to the ground within an inch of my life. It has turned out well and still I wrestle.

I am sitting on a porch, overlooking the Gulf of Mexico, and a young man is sprinting by. He reminds me of myself twenty years back: driving, wincing, pushing beyond the limits of reason to impress, even if it is only himself that he is impressing. He will tell the story of the pace of his run today to impress someone. It will work, if only in his own head.

It was easy being him once, driven by unfiltered piss and vinegar, tenacious, unflappable, somehow beyond certain of certain commitments. It was even easy morphing into him from unsure adolescence, faking it until you make it and then there comes a day when you aren't faking it anymore. They say that is when you have it made.

But the second puberty of moving into middle age isn't so easy. It feels something like retreating back into fakery, into acne and awkwardness. It feels like being stuck in the middle of all kinds of commitments and pseudo-commitments. All of a sudden, questions of how to even *be* retread their way into the forefront of your consciousness. This business of growing up human is not for the faint of heart.

This book is about all of that back and forth, all of that middling in between.

Ebenezer, the street where I saw the vision, or whatever it was, is a Hebrew word that means "stone of my help." In the Bible, the prophet Samuel set up a monument to commemorate a mighty victory over the Philistines, and he named it Ebenezer in reference to divine intervention. We will see.

1

The Middle: Home
By Another Way

The Lord called to Abram, "Go from your country, your people and your father's household to the land I will show you. I will make you into a great nation, and I will bless you; I will make your name great, and you will be a blessing. I will bless those who bless you, and whoever curses you I will curse; and all peoples on earth will be blessed through you." So Abram went, as the Lord had told him. Abram was seventy-five years old when he set out from Harran.—Genesis 12:1–4

"Even through his thick lenses, you can read the look of faith in his eye, and more than all the kosher meals, the ethical culture societies, the shaved heads of the women, the achievements of Maimonides, Einstein, Kissinger, it was that look that God loved him for and had chosen him for in the first place."—Frederick Buechner

I WAS RUNNING ALONG a network of hiking trails in middle Georgia. It was getting dark. I was six, seven miles in. The woods all looked the same. There were no signs, no landmarks. The terrain was as flat as a farm, and the pines as tall as you can imagine, so you couldn't see beyond your little patch. The darkness in these woods was unspeakable. It set in like a plague. Without the full moon, I wouldn't have had a prayer of getting out.

Everywhere I turned, deer shuttered and bolted from within the pines, sensing my intrusion. I could only hear them, branches rustling and footsteps. Every hunter I knew in town had stories of bear encounters on these trails. I was trying not to rouse them, wherever they were. My pace was Olympic, fueled by fear. It felt like I was running through some uncharted jungle, trying to stay a step ahead of the cannibals.

My journey had a starting point and I will discover its finish. For now, though, I'm just middling through the woods of middle Georgia.

We moved to middle Georgia from Atlanta just six months previously, a move much more dramatic than it sounds. In Atlanta, I was on the pastoral staff of a large and influential church where I had a lot of roots and a bright future. I loved my church, loved my coworkers, loved my life. I preached to thousands and loved the status. I loved being the first to the office and the last to leave. My girls were babies. I was writing my doctoral dissertation. I was asked to speak all over the place. The good days there still count as the most idyllic time of my professional and personal life.

Then my shiny yacht started taking on water. It was imperceptible at first because frankly, I was really popular. In any profession, especially those involving public roles, there are snipers on the periphery. But you only know they are there when you are shot or at least shot at. My assassin was right out in the open, carefully constructing an elaborate trap that he meant to catch me in, right in front of my face. He barely tried to hide. I did not handle it well. I knew I wasn't handling it well when I called him a dirty name and told him to go to hell, given that I am a Christian pastor.

Up to this point, the momentum of my life pulled forward under the weight of my own effort, seemingly under my inevitable, perfect control. I did the things that people do to build a polished resume. I was young and successful. I was most certainly privileged, whether I recognized it or not.

Now, for the first time, I couldn't achieve my way out of the situation. The handwriting was on the wall, my executioner aligning my fate, and I had babies to feed. I found a small church a hundred miles away in middle Georgia that would have me. I quit the big church on one Sunday, then preached in my new church the next. It was a heartbreaking necessity to stay a step ahead of the cannibals.

My wife and I had lived our entire adult lives in Atlanta and Chicago, so I thought the shift to small-town living would do us some good. The air was cleaner, the cost of living cheaper, the pace much slower. We were completely unprepared for the change. We moved a hundred miles and it was as exotic as the Amazon, but for all the wrong reasons. This middle Georgia town was a place that people moved from, not to.

Atlanta doesn't really have any nuances. It's like Houston with humidity: restaurant chains, strip malls, IT jobs. Atlanta is not the South. Moving to middle Georgia was like stepping into a Flannery O'Connor novel: you could feel the complexity in the air, the layered nature of everything. The codes were unspoken, but as real as language itself. Who you looked at, who you spoke to and how you did it, the way you knew when you had been affronted and how you were to respond, all governed by laws that might as well be commandments, except they were kept secret. Outsiders were held in high suspicion, and there we were, gringos, or, more accurately, foreign spies.

Pastoral ministry there submerged me in the particular dysfunctions of the rural, working-class South. The town had a series of desirable areas over the decades, each going to pot right after the other as the white people fled the black people. The vestiges of Jim Crow weren't even vestiges, as if no one received the memo about Martin Luther King, about modernity. In casual conversation, people referred to employees as "my Mexican" or "my boy." Like I said, it was different than Atlanta and Chicago.

Many of the people I ministered to seemed to lack a sense of agency, of being. They hadn't given a second thought to resume building. Life just happened to them. I prayed for unemployed people to find good jobs, they would work a month, then fail a drug test. I visited young men who would hole up in ratty hotels to drink for a week at a time. My worship leader went to jail for street fighting. I visited him.

Our work there bore some fruit, but it was a struggle. The church couldn't really afford to pay its bills, or me. Wounds within families that had been left untended for generations had an effect on the congregation's sense of hope. The people were lovely to us, but it just never felt like home, because it wasn't. As nice as people were, we were transplants, outsiders. We were stuck in the middle of our own story which happened to also land us in the middle of middle Georgia, trying to find our way. Our middle was geographic, professional, spiritual, existential. We were vagabonds, visibly and invisibly, trying to make our way home.

The truly seminal story in the Bible is surprising to most folks, even religious folks. It isn't creation and the Garden of Eden or King David or even Easter. It's an obscure story of God deciding on a particular nomad through whom to begin the nation of Israel, through whom God would rescue the world. We have no reason to differentiate him from other ancient near eastern nomads. There is no mention of his character, such as in the preceding story of Noah. His name means Big Papa, though he had no children, which made him a disgrace. For that matter, I supposed he was a laughingstock, like a guy named Farmer who didn't own any land.

That's really all we know. He was presumably worshipping the variety of ancient near eastern gods that folks in the region worshipped, and suddenly a different God chose the laughingstock, the disgrace. "The Lord called to Abram," Genesis 12:1 says. The Talmud names him "the first of the proselytes," and his evangelist was God himself. The people snickered, and the Lord called. In the Bible, the Lord tends to buck the system.

The promise that the Lord makes to Abram is beyond remarkable: "I will make you into a great nation, and all the nations of the earth will be blessed by you." Heavens to Betsy, you're just minding your own arid business one day when some offbeat deity appears and says, "I have decided that you will be the rescuer of the entire planet." It would have been sufficiently ridiculous had God called misfit Abram to rescue the neighborhood. "All the peoples of the earth"? A second earlier, Abram had been thinking about the food stuck in his teeth. There is no indication that he (or hardly anyone else at the time) had been a worshipper of this Lord. There is no indication that he even knew who the Lord was. And lest you think he was some model of piety, in the next story, we will see that he prostitutes his innocent wife to the Egyptians to save his own skin. "I have come not to call the righteous, but sinners," Jesus declared once. The Lord's HR department is obviously pretty lax.

But against the backdrop of this rather insane promise are the details. The promise is the promise, but there is a method by which it must be accessed. "Go from your country, your people, and your father's household to the land I will show you." Leave all that you have known and everything that is familiar, this at a time when most people probably hardly traveled further than twenty miles from the place of their birth. Thousands of years later, an anonymous New Testament author declared that Abram "obeyed and went, even though he did not know where he was going." I failed to mention that Abram was seventy-five years old at the time.

At seventy-five, God calls him to a new life in the middle.

There would be no fulfillment of the promise, no future nation, no blessing of all the earth's peoples if Abram was unwilling to depart from familiarity, from comfort, from certainty. I have seen this slogan thrown around on bumper stickers and such: "Not all who wander are lost." I have no idea what that means. When you are wandering around with no clear destination, you might as well be lost. I imagine that Abram felt the depths of lostness, traipsing around the desert with no clue where he might wind up. All he had was the promise of the renegade God who had called him "to the land I will show you."

In the middle, you either die or depend. And if you depend on the right things, the right things within you die. This has to be something of what Jesus meant when he declared that "He who loses his life for me will find it." You don't get new life without leaving the old one. You don't get new anything without braving the middle, not knowing where exactly it will lead.

Yet our culture spurns the middle. We are taught to know where we are going, sure as sugar, to create vision statements and retirement plans. "Where do you see yourself in five years?" is standard in job interviews. Know your destination, land on the shore, and burn the ships so that you can only move forward to the goal. Even in our churches, we hear legends of missionaries who set out for the Amazon with nothing but their coffins, so hardened was their certainty. Uncertainty is weakness. The life of strategy, of linear forward movement, is what is prized. And so we are taught that the middle is a place of mediocrity, a place for the wimps of this world.

But I just don't think that's true. I think the middle is a place of transformation. Sometimes the middle is, in fact, its own end. The way, it turns out, doesn't just have a middle, but it is the middle. "Rationality squeezes out much that is rich and juicy and fascinating," Annie Lamott writes.[1] The middle is largely irrational.

Abram eventually learned that it's in the woods, lost and running, where the promise lies.

1. Lamott, *Bird by Bird*, 112.

2

Reliances: The Middle Form

"Abram traveled through the land as far as the site of the great tree of Moreh at Shechem. At that time the Canaanites were in the land. The Lord appeared to Abram and said, 'To your offspring I will give this land.' So he built an altar there to the Lord, who had appeared to him."—Genesis 12:6–7

"There is a relation between the hours of our life and the centuries of time. As the air I breathe is drawn from the great repositories of nature, as the light on my book is yielded by a star a hundred millions of miles distant, as the poise of my body depends on the equilibrium of centrifugal and centripetal forces, so the hours should be instructed by the ages and the ages explained by the hours."—Ralph Waldo Emerson

I WAS RUNNING ALL over the place, just raking in the miles. My wife and I took a trip to northern California, run ten miles in the morning, eat breakfast, bike another twenty, then swim. We followed this routine for days and just couldn't get enough. I got back home and fell into the habit of running ten miles after dinner, endorphins making it then hard to fall asleep. But it is a feeling like no other, that runner's high, nature's opioid. I know that to nonrunners, this all seems nuts, but there really is an ease to it when you are in the groove.

And then, pain. I have never broken a bone, torn an ACL, or been sidelined for more than a few days with a sprain. But this was suddenly real pain. The pain started with an electric shock that I sometimes felt in the palms of my hands. It ended with a bruised right heel that was excruciating. After almost twenty years of running without incident and without much thinking about it, it now hurt to walk. I laid off of it for over a month, which made me miserable.

Up until this point, I had given no thought to *how* I was running. I had never heard there was a correct way. I had never been to one of those running stores that sold the name-brand shoes (too expensive). Finally, I went to a fancy running store in Atlanta. A young man with a plastic leg (not kidding) attended to me. He took me to the parking lot, recorded me running with his iPad, played it back in slow motion, and diagnosed the problem. "You're heel-striking," he said bluntly. "See how you are stretching out your entire leg and landing upward on your heel?" I watched the video, where I looked like a bounding animal of the grassland, springing up in huge, jaunty strides. "If you want to keep running, you better stop heel-striking," he warned. "Otherwise, get a bike."

I didn't want to get a bike, and I didn't want to hear a man with a plastic leg tell me to get a bike. Bikes are for old guys and you have to wear those embarrassing spandex outfits right out in public (who decided this was acceptable?). Some of them even shave their legs. So if I wanted to run like a man and hold onto a reasonable level of self-respect, I was going to need to figure this out.

They have classes on running form, but as an avowed Southern individualist I didn't want to mess with those. So I set out to change my running stride on my own. I figured that I would fix the problem by landing on the balls of my feet. That is the opposite end of the foot than the heel, after all. My heels thus protected, I would be back on the track to running bliss.

It was awful.

Yes, I stayed off my heels. But after a few miles, my calves were so over-exerted from the forward landing on the front of my foot that it felt like a knife stabbing each of them at every step. This was not going to work. I gave in and saw a running coach.

He put me on the treadmill and needed no more than thirty seconds. "Take small steps and stop stretching out," he said. "Land on the mid-foot."

I tried it and it was transformative. I was back and, years later, I now run without the pain that was routine in my thirties. Turns out that the key to this game is how you structure your landing. Land on the front or back of your foot, and you're soon done for. Land in the middle, the mid-foot, and you're off to the races.

Your running requires some structure, and sooner or later life does too. It requires the need to balance, take smaller strides, and to land solidly. It requires working with that solidity, not against it. It requires something beyond your own unique individuality. In the middle, that individuality tank eventually runs dry. It will leave you landing on your heel. As David Brooks writes, "If you make yourself, as William Ernest Henley's poem 'Invictus' put it, 'master of my fate . . . captain of my soul,' you are headed for the rocks."[1] In the middle, you figure out that you don't have it figured out. You look for handles. You look for voices. You look for community. Life in the middle requires structure, substance beyond yourself, just to stay off the cliffs.

My last book was about growing up in fiery Pentecostal churches in the South, when the life of faith was sweat, heat, and enchantment, and trying to make sense of all that as a young adult who pursued a high-brow education. Our church services back then—the center of our lives—were like NASCAR rallies, visceral and raucous. Everything formal was just the pregame show to the altar call, where anything might happen. You might see an angel, you might speak in tongues, God might knock you to the ground. It was personal, subjective, experiential, mystical, thunderous. And if you are wondering, yes, I do think it was real, though who really controls that definition?

---

1. Brooks, *The Second Mountain*, 254.

Then I became a pastor who people call Doctor at one of those respectable, affluent white-bread evangelical churches with loud rock music and fancy lights where the mahogany pulpit has been replaced with a hip stool from Pottery Barn. We turned the house lights down low like it was a concert, gave a snappy sermon, and we were done in an hour. It was like going to church at J. Crew, greeters and all. We filmed it and put it on the Internet every week. I loved these people with all my heart, I loved our beautiful faith, and I suffered through these trappings. On the big holidays, I wrapped a scarf around my face and sneaked off to Mass, which felt like a dangerous and rapturous Latin affair, and most Sundays, with the speakers blaring, I remembered Annie Dillard writing that she converted to Catholicism "solely to escape Protestant guitars."[2]

What I want to say is that all this "relevant" church is just like growing up Pentecostal, but without the participation. It's the same in that you are left to interpret and appropriate this experience for yourself. It is faith stripped of history. It's all the subjectivity without the thunder and, in many ways, without the community. And if you are wondering, yes, I do think it is real, though who really controls that definition?

In the middle, my individual interpretation of the purpose of life doesn't seem like a privilege. It seems airy. In the middle, we search for substance, we adjust our stride for solid ground to steady us. And what we need the most in the middle, what transforms quicksand into solid ground, is *history*.

"Abram traveled through the land as far as the site of the great tree of Moreh at Shechem," the story tells. This is literally the next Hebrew sentence after the almost-octogenarian obeyed God and set out from his homeland. He makes it to some tree that everybody talked about, the great tree where the sidewalk ends. There is a story about a group of Roman soldiers who were exploring the outskirts of the empire somewhere around Britain. "Send new orders," they wrote back to Rome via courier. "We've marched off

---

2. Dillard, *Teaching a Stone to Talk*, 23.

the map." Abram makes it past the tree that everyone told stories about, past the edge of the map.

Keep in mind that up until this point, a whopping six verses into the story of Abram, he is running on the fumes of a voice inside his head. "The Lord called to Abram" in verse 1, interrupting and disrupting his life, but it was only a voice. He took his clan with him, but only Abram had heard the voice. It was an individual journey. Abram ran out in front, alone.

And then, thunder. "The Lord appeared to Abram," the next sentence says. Not just a voice but a vision. Now God takes up space, geography, history. "To your offspring I will give this land," He says, reiterating the original promise. It is past the great tree, at the edges of the map, where the promised land begins. The voice leads you into Narnia, into the uncharted, and that's where the gods start showing up. Even Jesus learned this when "the Spirit drove him out into the desert" to meet the demons and God before anyone even knew about him.

What would you do if God appeared to you? You might write an account of the scene, but Abram was illiterate. You might call your pastor, but Abram didn't have one. You might get your life together, but whatever life Abram had, he had left behind. What Abram did have available was rocks.

"So he built an altar there to the Lord, who had appeared to him." I'm sure Abram struggles to understand the Lord, so he does one thing that he understands. He takes rocks and builds an altar. The story doesn't say that he does anything with it, just that he builds it. His former gods had altars, so he figures this made sense. He makes sure the moment matters, the moment will be remembered.

Abram builds an altar to live into history, to convert personal experience to something concrete. He builds the altar to mark the history, to join the history, and to leave the history for others. He takes a subjective moment and builds something objectively permanent. Now the vision has a story to be passed down. The vision has handles. The experience has substance. People have to deal with it, make of it what they will.

We need more altars in our lives, especially in the middle. They can save us from the isolation of getting lost in ourselves. They make us deal with things, important things. They provide structure that can ground and save us. So when you make it to the middle, above all, seek a history.

All of my redneck friends in Georgia are Anglican now, which would be a good book title for a recovering Pentecostal. It's true. The people I grew up with who used to try to speak in tongues now pray prayers that are prescribed by the liturgy. They honor the sacraments. They pay attention to the scaffolding of the church calendar. They have a priest. Heck, the members of my favorite punk rock band from when I was a teenager are now Greek Orthodox clerics. The coolest tech entrepreneur I know is a Russian Orthodox deacon, and he is a white boy from the suburbs. What to make of this crazy turn of events?

Really, it's pretty predictable. Over time, it just gets tiring trying to figure out the purpose of your life all on your own. In the long term, it's not realistic to follow the lone voice and to expect others to believe you because you say so. Eventually, you need something more concrete than that. Eventually, you need an altar to visit that says others have gone before you, so you aren't completely crazy. In the middle, you decolonize your identity, you unlayer. You start to crave some history to stand behind. In the middle, you find firmer reliances.

Lauren Winner was an observant Jew who became an Anglican Christian in college. She hated the evangelicals with their lack of anything beyond personal experience and whimsical interpretation ("What does this biblical passage mean to you?"), but loved what she deemed the familiarity of liturgy in Anglicanism. "Anglicans look at Scripture through the scrim of the church fathers, they balance the Bible with the weight of centuries of church teaching and tradition." It felt like Judaism to her, adorned with the beauty of Jesus and movement. Winner writes:

> The other familiar thing, when I first walked into an
> Episcopal church, was the prayer book, the habit of

fixed-hour prayer, the understanding that you were saying more or less the same liturgy as Anglicans around
the world, that you would say the same prayers every
morning, every evening, over and over and over, till
you knew them by heart, and long after that, till they
were rote and boring, comfortable as your best friend's
kitchen and familiar as flapjacks.[3]

Along with Winner, I happen to have found my history in the
depths of the church, where historical rootedness is pretty plug-
and-play. If the church is not your way, eventually, you're going to
want to find some history somewhere. History is an antidote to the
lostness of the soul that can take over in the middle. It is interesting
that two sentences after Abram builds the altar, after trekking even
further off the map, he builds another one. This time there was no
cue, no divine vision. He just builds it to build it. In the middle,
you are just lost without history, so you better double down.

You can find history in your family tree and legends, in a cause
that captures your heart, in a creed, in a mission beyond yourself.
History is something that can include you but that is also going to
go on regardless of you. History is the landing on the mid-foot, a
stride upon which you can rely. You don't get many reliances at all
throughout life, and in the middle, you might only get one.

Choose well and keep running.

---

3. Winner, *Girl Meets God*, 138.

3

Heresies: The Lies I Have Believed

Now there was a famine in the land, and Abram went down to Egypt to live there for a while because the famine was severe. As he was about to enter Egypt, he said to his wife Sarai, "I know what a beautiful woman you are. When the Egyptians see you, they will say, 'This is his wife.' Then they will kill me but will let you live. Say you are my sister so that I will be treated well for your sake and my life will be spared because of you."—Genesis 12:10–13

"Above all, do not lie to yourself. A man who lies to himself and listens to his own lie comes to a point where he does not discern any truth in himself or anywhere around him, and thus falls into disrespect towards himself and others."—Fyodor Dostoevsky

THAT NIGHT WHEN I was running from the cannibals through the woods of middle Georgia, I did not have a phone with me and there seemed to be no getting out. I climbed up a deer stand when there was still a hint of daylight, trying to find some marker to go by, but it was just endless woods in every direction. I thought about just spending the night up there and figuring things out in the morning, but I knew that my wife would, at some point, be in a panic, and then I would be on the news. As a new pastor in a smaller town, this was not the first impression that I wanted to make.

14

I had an old iPod Nano with me and I was listening to my favorite album from Band of Horses while I tried to run my way out. Seven or eight miles in, the battery ran out. That's when things started to get dicey.

Sometimes it's only in the silence that you realize how much we fill our lives with noise. I'm even convinced that noise is the fuel for our culture of consumerism. Noise doesn't create humans, but unthinking drones. Noise makes us mindlessly buy things, mindlessly spend our lives. In the nineteenth century, Soren Kierkegaard said that if he could prescribe a single cure for the illnesses of the modern world, it would be silence.[1] To his point, I have this dream that church could be an oasis of silence where we really deal with who we are, but our worship services now operate like radio stations, where "dead air" is anathema. If you really want to flee the noise, go to the woods.

I have run a marathon without stopping, so I know what I'm capable of. But just eight miles in, with no music in my head, the voices started to take over. I envisioned the worst. Like Leonardo DiCaprio in *The Revenant*, I just a knew that a bear was around the next bend, waiting to tear my guts out. I just knew that I was a few steps away from a shattered femur. I just knew that I would pass out from thirst and never get out. I just knew.

The reality is that I was on a soft and cleared trail that was constantly used by hunters. There was nothing to trip on. The reality is that if push came to shove, the hunters would be out on these trails early the next morning, in just a few hours. The reality is that if I just kept going, which I certainly could do, I would find some portal, some street, some option. But when you are in the middle, reality is often skewed. In the middle, it's not the lies that you have heard from other people that are crippling, but the lies that you tell yourself.

In 1988, Donald Lowry was an unknown and washed up middle-aged writer in the quad cities area of Western Illinois. Then, as can happen in middle age, he happened upon the idea of

1. Kierkegaard, *For Self-Examination*, 47.

a lifetime. Lowry began to notice that there were plenty of men across the country, young and old, who, just like him, were pretty unsuccessful in life and love, which had forced them into a pit he knew well, the pit of loneliness. To meet this growing market, he invented a mail-in subscription service where men could have a fantasy model pen-pal. The scams before the internet were so much more creative.

As his business began to get off the ground, Lowry hired real models to pose as these pen-pals, and he became quite sophisticated in building a comprehensive fantasy world around them. There were eight of them and they were called "the Angels" who lived in a fantasy town called Chonda-Za. I'm serious. They not only sent letters, but mementos of love and pictures for their pen-pals to carry in their wallets. They even sometimes made cassette tapes to send. Of course, it was beer-bellied Lowry who was doing most of the writing, impersonating the Angels from Chonda-Za. According to court documents, when Lowry was sentenced to 125 years in prison, his fraudulent scheme had taken in almost five million dollars.

I listened to a first-person account of one of the victims named Jesse and, as ridiculous as the whole scheme was, my heart really went out to him. He was a man in his forties who lived with his parents, had never had a girlfriend, was chronically overweight, and was probably on the margins of being mentally handicapped. His pen-pal was named "Angel Pamela," and they wrote back and forth for years, before Jesse finally proposed to meet her in person. Seizing the business opportunity, Lowery had already created a means for face-to-face meetings between the clients and the Angels. He staged little conferences where these paid actresses would show up and meet their pen-pals. And when Jesse arrived to meet his angel, he found a dozen other men also there to meet Pamela, each of them thinking that they were the singular object of her affection. He almost died that day, of a broken heart.

Of course, any rational person should have been able to tell that this was a farce. Yet that doesn't take away from the power of that moment with the twelve men, that feeling of realizing that you've been lying to yourself for years, to the point that you are convinced of things that aren't true. I'm convinced that it's in the middle of things—middle age, the middle of pain, loss, etc.— where we come face to face with our heresies, with the lies that we have believed.

Thus far in Genesis 12, there isn't much happening beyond the overarching plot of Abram's living in the foreign land of God's promise. Abram has built some altars, but mostly he has just walked around. Apart from obeying the voice and the vision, we know nothing of his character. That is about to dramatically change. Prepare to be disappointed.

"Now there was a famine in the land, and Abram went down to Egypt to live there." To say the least, this is unexpected. After risking it all on a whisper, after braving past the tree, after possessing the unknown land of promise, Abram suddenly races south, back to the map. No prayer, no altars, no submission, just fear that the Lord was unable to provide food and had hung him out to dry. The voice of fear became louder than the voice of promise, so Abram panicked. And ask any therapist, the voice of fear will always lead to craziness. In the middle, we can get distracted and jumpy.

What happens next, in modern terms, is that Abram perfectly rationalizes starting a little side hustle as a pimp. His wife, even at sixty-five, is apparently an uncommon beauty, one of "four beautiful women in the world" according to the Talmud. Abram quickly realizes that in Egypt this is a liability. So he pawns her off to Pharaoh and he gets paid. "Pharaoh treated Abram well for her sake, and Abram acquired sheep and cattle, male and female donkeys, menservants and maidservants, and camels." You start to see why Mark Twain said that if the public libraries are going to censor inappropriate literature, they sure as sugar better take the Bible off of their shelves. This part of the story didn't make it into the Sunday School children's song. Father Abraham had many sons . . . and also a profitable escort business. When

Pharaoh is your customer, your little brothel is going to do well. Those government checks don't bounce.

But remember that the Lord fell in with Abram in the first place because he was marginalized, so it's not surprising that He is bemused by this situation. "But the Lord inflicted serious diseases on Pharaoh and his household because of Abram's wife Sarai." Nobody else seemed to give a hoot about Sarai's wellbeing, so the Lord busted through the palace door like the FBI to shut down the front. Poor Sarai. The capitulation to the voice of fear, the lies that we believe, always have unwitting victims.

After I finished my doctoral degree, I started to have a little money. This was unexpected. I've always had a head for investing and we had been stable, but now I had some extra. I had this newfound time since I was no longer writing my dissertation, so I started teaching as an adjunct professor in a few places, started a small consulting outfit, published some books and articles, etc. Things really moved along, and I liked it. I got a decent car for the first time, we got to travel, we even bought a second house in the mountains. Stuff was cheaper then than it is now, so maybe I was good at it or just lucky or a bit of both.

Jesus had a lot to say about money, almost none of it good. Some would say he talked about it more than any other subject, which is really curious. God takes all that trouble to bend history around the arrival of Christ, and when he appears on the scene he wants to talk about your checkbook in between all of the healing and resurrecting and water-walking. Seems rather banal.

What's even weirder is that Jesus is markedly fanatic about the subject, like a messianic Dave Ramsey. You may have heard one of Ramsey's most famous shticks on the radio, where he has people come into the studio and scream bloody murder about being debt free. It strikes me as a bit over the top to travel to Nashville just to scream, but ok. My point is that Jesus went to similar extremes.

It would take a book series to scratch the surface of all Jesus had to say about money, so I'll just pick one spot. "No one can serve two masters," he says in the Sermon on the Mount in Matthew 6.

"Either he will hate the one and love the other, or he will be devoted to the one and despise the other." Makes sense. You can't split your allegiance down the middle, Jesus says, and you think that maybe he is talking about good and evil, or the devil, or being faithful to your political party. Then, he drops the bomb. "You cannot serve both God and money." Lord, we must discuss.

I understand putting God first; it's the hate language that is so troubling, the dualism. John Wesley, that Anglican preacher on horseback who touched off America's Great Awakening and founded the Methodist Church, famously said: "Give me one hundred preachers who fear nothing but sin and desire nothing but God, and I care not a straw whether they be clergymen or laymen, such alone will shake the gates of hell and set up the kingdom of heaven on earth."[2] But that's not what Jesus said. For that matter, Jesus nowhere tells anyone to hate sin, or to hate the devil. He clearly says to hate money, to despise it. The language is emotive.

I think Jesus said this because he knew that having money is often a cushion for the lies we tell ourselves. Yes, we might believe the lies without money, but money makes it easier. In middle age, you come to realize this.

The greatest lie we tell ourselves, of course, is that money will make us happier, more fulfilled, more purposeful. This is, proverbially, a hollow shell. The field of positive psychology has proven through research that happiness levels hardly budge after someone earns more than around $75,000 per year. The person with $75 million is typically no happier than the person with $75,000 and that is science. And Hollywood, with its rehab clinics and routine suicides, is little more than an ongoing exhibit of this materialistic lie. Still, the message is as attractive as the Angels in Chonda-Za, making contentment quantifiable. But it doesn't work.

Here's what's strange: When I started earning some extra money, the voices started. It is hard to describe, but very real. I did not hear these voices when I was younger, but suddenly they were upon me. They told me that I was worthless. They told me I was a quintessential failure. They told me I was an imposter. All

2. Tyerman, *The Life and Times of John Wesley*, 632.

evidence to the contrary! And what's wild is that the more successful in worldly terms that I became outwardly, the louder the voices became. I felt at times like one of the demoniacs that Jesus exorcised, just wanting the voices to go away.

I had breakfast with my wife at a restaurant and spilled all that had been building up inside of me. And then I said fateful words in a choke of tears with eggs in my mouth: "Extra money doesn't make the voices go away." There, I said it. I am telling you the truth: that was the day the voices stopped.

In the Gospel of Thomas, Jesus says, "If you bring forth what is inside you, what is inside you will save you. If you don't bring forth what is inside you, what you do not bring forth can destroy you."

Don't get me wrong, I still hear the echoes from time to time, but they aren't like the real thing. The imposter syndrome probably just goes with the territory of modest achievement, so you learn to manage it. But it's nothing like what it was. Somehow, just naming the lie that I had believed was all that it took to set me free. When you name something, you don't have to fear it anymore. Jesus once asked a bunch of demons, "What is your name?" and the man who they had in a stranglehold was set free.

We are all heretics. Sometimes it just takes some time for your heresies to fail you so that you can name them. Abram's heresy was that he thought the Lord had left him. Mine was that my worth is tied to a bunch of externals. Yours may be related to power, or sex, or adrenaline. The heresies seek you out, and they work for a time. Then you reach some middle passage where you realize Chonda-Za is not a real place. You have that moment where you come face to face with the lies that you have believed.

Listen to the voices, but don't heed them. Name them.

4

Loneliness: Running Out
of No-Man's Land

Now Lot, who was moving about with Abram, also
had flocks and herds and tents. But the land could not
support them while they stayed together, for their possessions were so great that they were not able to stay
together. And quarrelling arose between Abram's herdsmen and the herdsmen of Lot.—Genesis 13:5–7

"Anyone who believes that it is fairly easy to be the single
individual can always be sure that he is not a knight of
faith, for fly-by-nights and itinerant geniuses are not
men of faith."—Soren Kierkegaard

I DIDN'T START RUNNING competitively until my sophomore year
of college. I get bored easily, and I was sitting in a class learning
how to read ancient Greek literature when I noticed a green flyer
by the door. It said in bold letters, "Come Join the Cross Country
Team." I had never thought of this possibility before but had been
running on my own a good deal and figured I could do it. So I tried
out and made the team, even got a scholarship. Figuring out how
to succeed in the sport, though, was another matter.

In college, the race meets are large, typically hundreds of runners, and the length is five miles. One of the first benchmarks of
respectability is breaking the thirty-minute mark, which requires

going more or less all-out from the starting gun. In my first races, I came out at a blistering five-minute pace. In the second mile, I would settle in. Then I couldn't quite keep up. What's worse, in miles three and four I fell into a nasty habit. For whatever reason, I couldn't stay out of "No-Man's Land."

Running may seem to many like a solitary sport, but competitive running is actually a pack sport. Study after study shows that running with even one person increases performance. In competitive running, the name of the game is to find a group that suits your pace and then just keep up. Large races today will even have pacers that carry a big sign so that you can stick with the group that matches your finishing goal. My problem starting out in college running is that I chose a group in the early stage of the race that was too fast for me. In mile three, they would accelerate, and I would fall behind. In the middle of the course, I would be completely alone: no fans, no supporters, no teammates, no other runners in site. No-Man's Land. You do not want to be there.

At all costs, avoid No-Man's Land.

My friend Aaron and I have been close friends since high school, which makes it a friendship of thirty years. That itself feels weird to write, and we've lived a lot of stories. We played in several bands in our college days, toured a bit, recorded in some upscale music studios. There's a level of closeness in living out of a van to create art together that is hard to describe. We were not drinkers in college and yet would stay up all night on the weekends, just goofing off, watching Adam Sandler movies, playing video games. On the weekdays, we used to stay up all night studying together for major tests, keeping each other awake, surviving on gallons of sweet tea. Cicero, that great Roman orator, said, "Life is nothing without friendship." These are precious memories.

And then a few months ago, we buried Aaron's father. I flew into Houston to officiate the funeral. Aaron and I met at a Mexican restaurant the night before. I could only mutter one question: "Are we of the age where we bury our parents?"

Yes, because this is the middle.

Aaron is a pretty inspiring guy. He miraculously married up (trust me on this, I had a front row seat to his dating debacles) and has three kids. He and his wife work at a Christian school, which pays dirt, so he started his own successful company on the side. He volunteers at his church. As if all this weren't enough, he and Emily adopted a special needs daughter from China at vast expense. If you knew Aaron when he was young, you would also be inspired by this. He has come a long way.

Aaron asked to have lunch with me a few weeks ago, and something was different. He was quieter, far less manic, brighter in the eyes, something like a look of shock or wonder on his face. He had just returned from his very first mission trip with his church, working in one of the poorest communities in the Dominican Republic. He told me it was the greatest week of his life.

I mentioned the death of Aaron's father, which shouldn't have happened. Mental illness is a strain in Aaron's family, and at times even he has fended it off. I have seen that the pressures of this have made Aaron tense and distant at times, notwithstanding his graces. Like me, he is a fighter. But the fight can make you tired, lonely, walled off. He told me that on the mission trip, he finally recognized the thickness of those walls.

He was being led in the Ignatian Examination the last day of the trip, which is sort of like meditation, prayer, and self-exploration all in one, when he heard a voice. Only this wasn't one of the usual bad voices that you hear in the middle, but something different. He told me that he heard something say this: "You were created for community." He told me there is no way that came from him. He told me that for the first time, he heard the voice of God.

The Jesuit priest Karl Rahner said, "In the days ahead, you will either be a mystic, or nothing at all."[1]

It is natural to imagine that nomadic Abram is mostly alone, lost in the desert. But this isn't true. He has a vibrant community around him. And I'm not even referring to his own nuclear family, shepherds, employees and passersby. Turns out that Abram is also

---

1. Endean, *Karl Rahner and Ignatian Spirituality*, 63.

traveling with his nephew, Lot, who has quite a retinue himself. They may not know where they are heading, but they are heading there as a community, and I imagine that this is really important to making the whole venture work. It probably feels adventurous, like climbing Mount Everest in white-out conditions, continuing to move forward, depending on each other for lack of sight, dreaming of the promise. Nothing creates a sense of community like facing adversity together for the sake of a grand prize.

But then, trouble in the middle of the journey. Once again, the problem is money.

"The land could not support them while they stayed together, for their possessions were so great." This contention is patently ridiculous, reflecting their myopia. We are told two sentences later, "The Canaanites and Perizzites were also living in the land." That is, the land is supporting a wide array of clans. Let's not forget that it was the Lord himself who sent them to that very land, so it stands to reason that it could sustain an additional family or two. "The land is mine," God says elsewhere in the Torah, flatly.

They succumb to a scarcity mindset and it tears them apart. Community gives way to competition. They have so much stuff that they feared they won't have enough. That is the myth of wealth, the never-ending gluttony of capitalism, Rockefeller's famous need for "just a little bit more." Scarcity is common in the middle, because at its core, scarcity is what happens when we learn to withhold things, especially trust. A scarcity mindset allows you divide up the land so that you know what's yours, and you think it will protect you, and then you are all alone.

Back when I used to preach to thousands of people, I sometimes received standing ovations. It wasn't all the time, and it really wasn't what I was after. Preaching is like playing jazz, in that you have to be extremely committed to the craft for the magic to happen every now and then, but you can't just summons it up. If you aren't in it for the craft itself, you're not going to last, because you have to love putting the notes together for the sake of the art. Sometimes the notes just work and you lose yourself in them in a way that lifts people from themselves. Sometimes for a moment they transplant themselves into the story you are telling, a more hopeful story than what they imagined to be possible. My approach to preaching is not conveying new or helpful information; I'm trying to inspire something within. I am trying to break your heart.

One time this happened, and the roof lifted off of the sanctuary, and the people stood to their feet as one when I was finished, and they applauded for a good while, and I do not remember what I had been saying, but I remember feeling disconnected from the whole experience, like I was out of my body. I remember that their clapping seemed to be stirring the air up into waves, and the waves kept emanating toward me, washing over me. But what they brought was not appreciation or joy, but sadness. I just felt sadness wafting me over me, sadness that felt palpable, which was the opposite of what they meant, of course. I did not understand this, but I knew it was the culmination of a problem that had been brewing for some time. I knew that this sort of lack of connection with people who wanted to connect with me was a disease of the heart.

I went and met with a counselor who was recommended to me because he had also been a minister. I did not want to go. We spoke for a few minutes and he asked me a question: "Can I tell you what your entire persona gives off, your body language, your expression?" "Sure," I said. "When you walked in the room, it was like you were saying to the whole world, 'Don't mess with me.' Your walls are ten feet thick."

And I knew it was true. I had become a professional at withholding.

"Myself" was one of the first words my first daughter began to say before she was even a year old, which is typical of children, and I identified with her. For the first decades of life, I decided things for myself. My favorite poems were anthems of rugged individualism. "To strive, to seek, to find, and not to yield," in Tennyson's Ulysses. "Never look back and say, could have been me," by the Struts. These decades were characterized by competition—academic, athletic, social—and I won a lot. For heaven's sakes, faith in God was even individualistic! We used to sing a song in the Pentecostal church:

"What God has for me *it is for me*." Life was about my experiences and my achievements and withholding all of them from anyone who might encroach. "Myself!"

But this withholding begins to fail you in the middle.

We withhold because we don't want to lose things. We withhold because we become addicted to competition. We withhold because somebody took something that mattered to us once and we don't want that to happen again. We withhold because, like a boxer with his gloves in front of his face, we're sick of getting hit. So we retract into ourselves. We trade emotion for autism. I heard a preacher recently say that "the kind of loneliness that modernity engenders is not that of being stranded on a deserted island or sent abroad to a foreign country so much as it is an aloneness that resembles lostness, an aimlessness, disconnected and unrelated to others."[2] We try to make a home in No-Man's Land, thinking it is a safer there, and indeed it is, and it's miserable. C.S. Lewis said that this is the very definition of hell, an eternal withholding loneliness. It would be better to lose, better to live in the danger.

One of the more famous stories of Jesus is his healing of the lepers. It is sort of like Mahatma Gandhi ordering that everyone stop excluding the Untouchable caste in India, but perhaps more visceral than that. These skin diseases in the ancient world were serious business. Leviticus 13:45 prescribed the rule for these cases in Jesus' culture: "The person with such an infectious disease must wear torn clothes, let his hair be unkempt, cover the lower part of his face and cry out, 'Unclean! Unclean!'" There could be no facing them, no contact.

Often enough, Jesus heals with a word. "Go! It will be done just as you believe it would," he said to the centurion, healing his servant from miles away. When it comes to lepers, though, Jesus has to get his hands dirty. When it comes to the untouchable class, Jesus has to pick a fight with his own Bible, his own religion. In the preceding story, "Jesus reached out his hand and touched the man. 'I am willing,' he said. 'Be clean!'"

2. Curry, "With Head Held High," 4.

Imagine neither touching nor being touched for longer than you could remember. Imagine the isolation and loneliness. They literally lived in No-Man's Land, outside the village and cities, locked out of societies. The Bible said clearly not to touch them, but Jesus couldn't help himself. Some scholars have even said that the point is not the physical healing, whether it happened medically or not, but the social reinstatement. If the very Messiah touches you, then you are touchable for everyone else.

The night before his death, Jesus washed the feet of his disciples. One of them objected. Jesus drew the hardest line of his life. "Unless I wash you," he said, "You have no part with me." His touch is nonnegotiable. He is going to touch you even if his Bible says not to. He is going to touch you even if you don't want him to. He is going to touch you if it kills him. The only way you can avoid it is to run away into No-Man's Land.

In the very next Genesis story, the scarcity mentality that had caused Abram and Lot to break from community together enflames the entire region. Four kings go to war over land grabbing and Lot is captured for no other reason than he is wealthy and happens to live there now. Abram goes and rescues him, and one of the kings is so impressed that he offers Abram a blessing. Abram decides to peel off 10 percent of his net worth and give it to the king for no apparent reason other than gratitude. The restoration of community coincides with rejecting scarcity, with letting go.

The late Catholic priest Henri Nouwen once wrote that "our deepest human desire is to give ourselves to each other as a source of physical, emotional, and spiritual growth,"[3] like a sacred meal.

3. Nouwen, *Life of the Beloved*, 111.

5

Forgiveness: The Medicine of the Middle

"So Lot chose for himself the whole plain of the Jordan and set out toward the east. The two men parted company."—Genesis 13:12

"And grace is the great gift. So to be forgiven is only half the gift. The other half is that we also can forgive, restore, and liberate, and therefore we can feel the will of God enacted through us, which is the great restoration of ourselves to ourselves."—Marilynne Robinson, *Gilead*

FOR ME, RUNNING HAS been a means of inner peace, of sorting things out. There is something about the flow of it all that puts things in perspective, that orders disconnected thoughts. When Rabbi Abraham Joshua Heschel marched for civil rights with Dr. King, he said afterward that it felt like "my legs were praying." Yes.

But back when the job that I passionately loved was slowly trickling away, my running took a different form. Instead of a time to clear my head, running instead stoked the locomotive of bitterness. When I ran, I replayed scripts in my head of all of my justifications, and self-pity, and self-righteousness, and all of the ways I would get back at the trolls who wronged me. I replayed movie scenes in my head of storming out on my terms, of the perfectly cutting one-liners, of getting back at everyone. It was unhealthy, and it locked me up inside. What's dangerous about anger is that it can indeed be contained, and when contained, like nuclear energy, it just keeps re-sparking upon itself. It never dies out.

About six miles in on one of these bitterness runs, I ran by a little podunk Baptist Church. There are so many in the South that we don't even notice them anymore, like pine trees. I had probably run by this same church a thousand times. It had one of those marquis signs to post inspirational messages for the community, which is one of the many odd things we Christian folk do. I cannot explain why on earth I read the sign that day, apart from a love so incomprehensible, it drives the smallest, most relatively insignificant things in the universe. The sign read, "Forgive everyone, everything."

Have you ever prayed for a sign from God?

It felt like someone was playing a prank on me, like I was being punked. I somehow expected my friends were about to jump out of the bushes with a camera, laughing and pointing. I literally ran forward a hundred yards when my curiosity got the better of me. Could this be one of those roadside "mystery spots" where gravity runs uphill, one of the "thin places" where the veil seeks to disappear? I turned around and ran back to the sign to make sure the message was still there. It would not have surprised me if it was blank the second time, but there it still was. "Forgive everyone, everything," like a slap in the face, like a kiss.

Who is this God, sneaking around, rearranging the letters on our chipper Baptist signs, tricking us toward grace?

I want to be careful about speculating on the feelings of ancient near eastern nomads, but they certainly did have them. These stories in Genesis are filled with pathos and tension. I would imagine then that Abram had some similar feelings of bitterness when Lot up and ditched him.

This region is still known as a hospitality culture, and this would have been even more pronounced in ancient times. In hospitality cultures, one's honor is bound up in extending oneself to strangers and friends alike. To refuse hospitality was to insult a man's honor. Lot did this to Abram when he left.

It must have especially stung, given that Abram took the high road when he certainly didn't have to. He could have smacked Lot in the mouth and been justified. His honor had been stomped upon in front of God and everyone. Lot might as well have cursed Abram's mother to his face. And though we have already seen that Abram was far from some paragon of virtue, he gets something right this time. He extends grace.

"Let's not have any quarrelling between you and me, or between your herdsmen and mine, for we are brothers," Abram contends. "Is not the whole land before you? Let's part company. If you go to the left, I'll go to the right; if you go to the right, I'll go to the left." Of course, Lot chose the more irrigated direction after this blessing from Abram. Lot withheld and grabbed. Abram let go.

I love what happens next.

"The Lord said to Abram after Lot had parted from him, 'Lift up your eyes from where you are and look north and south, east and west. All the land that you see I will give to you and your offspring forever.'" Abram's act of grace touches the very heart of God. The promise of grace is reiterated. Grace just explodes. St. John Chrysostom said many centuries ago, "The abundant grace we have received is not just a medicine sufficient to heal the wound of sin, but also health and beauty and honor, and glory and dignity." Resentment is, by definition, containment, but grace simply can't be contained. Grace is health, beauty, honor, glory, dignity. Like a virus, grace begets grace begets grace . . .

You may know what it is like to pray for a sign from God, some crystal-clear direction. One of the most bothersome dynamics of the Bible is the way God so speaks to people. Pharaoh has a dream, and Joseph tells him precisely what it means. The Hebrew prophets announce, "Thus saith the Lord," and just spew it all out. The Son of God preaches a sermon on a mount for whosoever to hear. And we typically just need a little clarity on things of far less import: Should I take that job? Should I date this person? Should I buy or rent?

And then God writes exactly what you need on a marquis sign on a run that you will never forget. And I must tell you that I ignored it. I didn't forgive anyone for anything, not a soul. I know this is nuts, but it's why even divine signs have limitations. The Israelites can look out of the tent to see God's very pillar of fire that they are following toward freedom and independence, and still, they beg to go back to slavery in Egypt. Jesus said, "A wicked and adulterous generation looks for a miraculous sign," even as he was spinning off miracles at will, healing bodies and wilting plants and putting coins into the mouths of fish underwater. At the most, then, signs from God are an invitation.

I ran past the sign, understood the invitation, but just moved on. In Marilynne Robinson's magisterial novel, *Gilead*, the pastor says, "I have always liked the phrase 'nursing a grudge,' because many people are tender of their resentments, as of the thing nearest their hearts." I know exactly what this means.

I moved to middle Georgia to the small church and eventually returned to a big one again. I finished my doctorate and kept full steam ahead. I had survived and overcome. But I was running with the exact same weight of conscious bitterness as before. It made no sense to me. I was a walking contradiction. I fought a lot of physical illnesses, including bouts of pneumonia. I was tired all the time. I was brusque with people. I needed professional help, and finally I sought it.

I did an internet search for a Christian counselor and found a guy who would take my insurance. He seemed normal enough: older than me, doughy, Catholic. I showed up for the appointment, my first ever of this nature, and it was as you would imagine: a leather couch, white walls, a window. I didn't want to do this, but I had paid the co-pay and it seemed dumb to quit before I had started. So I just let him have it.

For exactly fifty-five minutes, I poured it all out. Gave him my whole ascendant professional history and contrasted it with all of these negative feelings that I failed to understand nor control. How could life be going nothing but well and I still just wish I could walk into a motorcycle bar and bust some skulls like Samson the judge? It was just pure word vomit—no story arc, no focus—just scattering raw, disconnected experiences of disconnection.

I finished my hurling, and he sat back. A pregnant pause, then he spoke slowly. "Josh, here is what I want you to do. I want you to let go . . . and let G— . . ." And I am about to turn over his desk like Jesus in the Temple before he spits that last word out. I'm looking for a pen, a letter-opener, a shiv to stab him in the larynx like Jason Bourne before he says it. I want to plug my fingers in my ears and scream so that I don't hear it.

"Let go and let God."

In the South, we have these trite little phrases on bumper stickers and coffee mugs. I have seen "Let go and let God" on 1989 Honda Civics, right beside "My Boss is a Jewish Carpenter" and other such drivel. And I paid a licensed professional for this counsel.

I left a minute later, having no idea what to make of this. I examined his educational credentials, looked for a criminal record. Everything checked out. I went back. He said the same thing. He kept saying it. And finally, one day, I looked in the mirror, said it to myself, and came to see the person staring back at me: gripping the steering wheel of everything with white knuckles, gunning the engine, going, going, going, trying to outrun, to outpace the simple necessity that was eating away me like a bacterium: "Forgive everyone, everything."

"The descent into Hell is easy," the Roman poet Virgil wrote. "But to retrace your steps and to come out into the upper air, this is the deed, this is the labor."

In the middle, we retrace, we recede, but we will only ascend if we let go.

6

Blessing: Middle Words

Then Melchizedek king of Salem brought out bread and wine. He was priest of God Most High, and he blessed Abram, saying, "Blessed be Abram by God Most High, Creator of heaven and earth. And blessed be God Most High, who delivered your enemies into your hand." Then Abram gave him a tenth of everything.—Genesis 14:18–20

Today like every other day we wake up empty
And frightened. Don't open the door to the study
And begin reading. Take down a musical instrument.
Let the beauty we love be what we do.
There are hundreds of ways to kneel and kiss the ground.

—Rumi

I WAS RECENTLY RUNNING my common one-hour route early in the morning. I once heard a soundscape artist say that the most placid time of the day is 4:00 AM, and for me, there is no better time to be out. No traffic, no noise, just moonlight.

I turned a corner at the halfway mark, and suddenly a large man was a few dozen yards ahead of me, running like it was his first time. It was cold, and from what I could, tell he was dressed in a plush jumpsuit, like a car mechanic in the winter. He was running like a thunder god; no grace to his steps. I stepped into the street to pass him and we greeted each other. He was huffing like an

Olympic sprinter, stomping back and forth. He had a beard down to his chest. And just when the scene couldn't be much odder at four in the morning, he called out to me after I passed him.

"Jesus loves you."

Oh, the "Christ-haunted south," as Flannery O'Connor put it. Those trite words. I have never seen that man again. "Do not forget to entertain strangers," Hebrews 13:2 says, "for thereby some have entertained angels unaware."

I have no doubt that I was there that morning to receive those words of blessing.

There is no other sport that is built upon such intentional verbal encouragement than running. No, we aren't packing stadiums all that often like the NFL, but that's why I use the word *intentional*. Major sports events are plenty loud, but it is typically just a bunch of rabid shouting. People who work in jobs they hate all week get their own nice seat and a beer and have themselves a little catharsis on the weekend over a ball game. This doesn't happen at races.

The fans arrive early, often with posters they have made ("You can do it!"). They bring water and snacks to pass out. And they have something positive to say to every runner that goes by. I'm telling you they don't know you from Adam, and they look you right in the eye and smile and tell you how wonderfully able you are to do what you're doing. It's like every race is a beautiful day in Mr. Rogers' neighborhood, or like the liberal seminaries I attended. You can't believe that people who are this nice exist.

Not only that, at the community events, the runners are also this nice to each other. I have run a half-marathon in downtown Atlanta on Thanksgiving morning for many years, and the sweetest thing you have ever seen are the runners pushing their special needs children in a wheelchair. Their serotonin levels must just skyrocket the whole time with all of that affirmation. Every runner who passes them has a thumbs-up, a pat on the back. "Come on, runner!" we all shout as we go by, forgetting about the pain, everyone smiling from ear to ear. It's a taste of something, like church, and the feeling sticks with you. You remember it.

That feeling is what the ancients called a blessing.

Now we arrive at one of the most mysterious events of Abram's life. The meaning of it has been debated for decades. The buildup to this event is straightforward enough. There is a battle between a bunch of kings. Abram gets involved when he finds out Lot has been captured. Abram wins and Lot is rescued. Lot and all of his property are recovered and Abram has shored up the right alliances. And then a mystery that casts a shadow over multiple faiths appears and disappears.

His name was Melchizedek, the King of Salem and a priest. In the whole Hebrew Bible, he appears here for a moment, then, even weirder, in one line in a Psalm. Walter Brueggemann calls this "the most enigmatic chapter in Genesis"[1] because of the ephemeral Melchizedek. The earliest rabbinic interpretations argued that he was the first king of Jerusalem, honored in the text because he fed all of Abram's army with bread and wine. Later, the Dead Sea Scrolls call him the archangel Michael, arrayed in glory to judge the quick and the dead. I guess it's not surprising that the only reference to Melchizedek in the New Testament has him as a stand-in for Jesus, the ultimate high priest. But my favorite interpretation is from the later rabbis in the Talmud, those who draw from centuries of debate. To them, the point was the power of Melchizedek's blessing, which he screwed up. "But when Melchizedek put Abraham's blessing before God's own, God resolved to have the priesthood descend from Abraham instead." Melchizedek got the blessing wrong, so God gave it away.

This is the power of a blessing and it is no laughing matter. That is the point.

Yesterday I read an article about childhood trauma, the cold hard numbers of the percentage of children in our country who are maltreated, shoved aside, abused. It was horrifying in its scientific precision; just a bunch of nameless statistics. The researchers even totaled up the projected economic impact of

1. Brueggemann, *Genesis*, 134.

traumatized children in healthcare costs, educational struggles and lost professional productivity (dear heaven, we need an economics lesson to care?). It was like reading about some dystopian machine world, not about rapturous, innocent children who have intrinsic, infinite value.

There is a scholar in Israel (of all places) who writes about the history of humanity from a purely atheistic perspective. He points out that every major advancement during the modern era that we applaud comes from Christian ideas that are simply myths that allow us to generally cooperate with one another. Human rights are myths. Just laws are myths. Equality is a myth. Morality is a myth. And, of course, the foundation of all these things—God—is the ultimate myth. He takes specific issue with the American Declaration of Independence:

> According to the science of biology, people were not 'created'. They have evolved. And they certainly did not evolve to be 'equal'. The idea of equality is inextricably intertwined with the idea of creation. The Americans got the idea of equality from Christianity, which argues that every person has a divinely created soul, and that all souls are equal before God. However, if we do not believe in the Christian myths about God, creation and souls, what does it mean that all people are 'equal'? Evolution is based on difference, not on equality . . . 'Created equal' should therefore be translated into 'evolved differently.' Just as people were never created, neither, according to the science of biology, is there a 'Creator' who 'endows' them with anything. There is only a blind evolutionary process, devoid of any purpose, leading to the birth of individuals.[2]

We are, in the words of this scholar, "an animal of no significance."[3] This is the world that is coming, that is here, if blessing is also a myth, world without end.

But the biblical world is different, a world of its own that is itself world-producing. In the biblical world, the question is

2. Harari, *Sapiens*, 109.

3. Harari, *Sapiens*, 3.

not whether God created or whether evolution created. The first is so assumed that it is background, and the second is certainly not excluded. What is foreground is that this creative power lives in every moment. *Words have this creative power*, to bless or to curse. Like fire, words cannot be neutral.

By words, God spoke creation into existence. "Let there be light." By words, God gave Torah, commandments, and "thus saith the Lord" of the prophets. "In the beginning was the Word," the Gospel of John begins. In fact, the Hebrew word for *word* —*dabar*—is the identical word for *deed*. Words do, and to do is to speak. And the ultimate constellation of words, like a symphony, that can reach the apex of that creative power, is what the ancients called *blessing*.

Henri Nouwen writes that blessing is more than compliment or affirmation: "A blessing goes beyond the distinction between admiration or condemnation, between virtues or vices, between good deeds or evil deeds. A blessing touches the original goodness of the other and calls forth his or her Belovedness."[4] Blessing is sacred speech, like a baptism of words, an immersion in truth. In the middle of life, truth can so easily get murky. The words that we have heard over the years have piled up like plaque in our veins, conflagrating life. In the middle, blessing can give you back yourself.

That time when the assassin had set up a stakeout for me, I experienced a series of strange incidents. Our giant church had a small prayer chapel up in the inner workings that was almost always empty. I went up there each week to prepare sermons and to pray. One day, another man was praying in the back. I took a place up in the front and went about my business.

After a while, he broke the silence from the back: "You're Pastor Josh, aren't you?" By the way, you're really not supposed to talk in the prayer chapel. I can only paraphrase the middle part, and you would need to spend some time in a Pentecostal church to understand how it works. He had no knowledge of my

4. Nouwen, *Life of the Beloved*, 69.

situation but felt like the Lord wanted him to tell me that He saw what I was going through. I can quote the last phrase directly: "God's got your back."

I just love it, this dishwater blessing. It is so southern and charming and colloquial, like a book title that made its way to the convenience store, right beside "Chicken Soup for the Soul." The problem was that it didn't stop and kept getting freakier. People kept coming up to me out of the clear blue with the same message. The grand finale was a voicemail I received from a pastor 1200 miles away whom I hadn't spoken to in years. He said that I had arisen in his prayer time, then went on to describe my situation in detail, only to say at the end: "God wants you to know, He has your back. Bye."

He didn't even ask for me to call him back, just my own personal dial-up oracle. And I think this is the way the world really is, a world of everyday glory. I think the world is a place where some priest from Salem shows up out of nowhere and blesses your socks off. I think the world is enchanted, and that blessing trumps statistics every time.

Henri Nouwen left a teaching career at Harvard University and the global speaking circuit to care for the severely handicapped at the L'Arche Daybreak community in Toronto, where he spent the last ten years of his life. He tells the story of preparing to lead the mass for the community when one of the members interrupted his preparation to ask for a blessing. Distracted, he quickly made the sign of the cross on her forehead, but she would have none of it. "No, I want a real blessing!" she insisted.

In the middle of the mass, he put his arms around her, the white sleeves of his robe draping her face. "Janet," he said aloud,

> I want you to know that you are God's beloved daughter. You are precious in God's eyes. Your beautiful smile, your kindness to people in your house, and all the good things you do show us what a beautiful human being you are. I know you feel a little low these days and that there is some sadness in your heart, but I want you to remember

who you are: a very special person, deeply loved by God
and all the people who are here with you.[5]

When she smiled and sat down, someone else called out: "I want a
blessing too!" And the mass finally really happened because they
skipped it wholesale as one by one the handicapped just kept coming forward for their blessing.

    The Talmud says, "It is forbidden to taste of the pleasures of
this world without a blessing."

5. Nouwen, *Life of the Beloved*, 71.

7

Ecstasy: Monks and the Middle

Abram believed the Lord, and he credited it to him as righteousness.—Genesis 15:6

"Rabbi Mendel once boasted to his teacher Rabbi Elimelekh that evenings he saw the angel who rolls away the light before the darkness, and mornings the angel who rolls away the darkness before the light. 'Yes,' said Rabbi Elimelekh, 'in my youth I saw that too. Later on you don't see these things anymore.'"—Martin Buber

IT IS EASY TO imagine that distance running is largely an American, or at least western, enterprise. After all, it is a solitary sport, and we happen to be the most individualistic nation in history. The advent of the Nike running shoe, popularized by the founder's memoir, *Shoe Dog*, certainly contributed to this sensibility. But it isn't true. We just made it into a sport, into a competition as we do all things in the West. What if I told you that, at its origins, running is more like prayer, like an entrance into the divine realm?

More than a generation ago, a documentarian countered the Nike-fueled American craze of running with a short film that was little noticed at the time. For that matter, the opening narration questions the entire Western foundation of the "marathon" as the peak of running achievement:

> The ultimate test of human athletic endurance is the
> marathon, a twenty-six mile cross-country dash reflect-
> ing the achievement of a Greek messenger in the year 490
> B.C. Today the unrivaled champions of this endeavor are
> not the professional stars, but an order of Tendai Bud-
> dhist monks whose monastery is in central Japan. They
> are the marathon monks of Mount Hiei.[1]

Since 1885, dozens of Tendai Buddhist monks in remote
central Japan have attempted a feat that is ultimate to their faith
and worldview: the completion of a seven-year range of 1,000
marathons totaling 27,000 miles, greater than the complete cir-
cumference of the equator. If that doesn't sound intimidating to
you, take all this in:

The first test requires one hundred days of consecutive eigh-
teen-mile runs that begin at midnight. They typically last eight
hours because of the darkness and the difficult terrain. The monk
can sit down only once during the trek to pray for two minutes.
The trail is built around the five peaks of Mt. Hiei, the tallest of
which is almost 3,000 feet. It is lush and sweltering in the summer,
snowy in the winter. Oh, and the monk has to wear sandals hand-
made of straw. And if he fails, he must kill himself.

If he makes it through the hundred days, he can apply to
be tested by the remaining 900 marathons over the next seven
years. In the fourth year, he is allowed to wear socks, but the distance doubles: 200 consecutive days of marathons for years four
and five (thank you, socks). In the sixth year, again the distance
doubles. In the seventh year, the 200-day runs are two marathons
(fifty-two miles) each day. He will sleep two hours per day. The
faithful come to the trails, and he will bless their heads with
prayer beads along the way.

During the seventh year, there is an even greater batch of
required prayers, offerings, funerary rites, and omens, including
a seven-day period of meditation in which the monk cannot eat,
drink, sleep or stand up. Some can handle the running but die during the meditation.

1. Hayden, *Marathon Monks of Mount Hiei*. DVD.

The goal of all this? Nirvana. Enlightenment. Ecstasy. To lose themselves in the mountain, the earth itself. It is said that by the seventh year, they can hear the ash falling off of an incense stick, can feel the pores of their body drinking in the mist. The authoritative book on the running monks of Mount Hiei ends with their transformation: "Facing death over and over, the marathon monks become alive to each moment, full of gratitude, joy and grace."[2]

Another Eastern mystic once said, long before, "He who loses his life will find it."

The story of Abraham is really long. That may seem insignificant, but think about how long it is and how little of Abraham's story is told. Entire chapters are devoted to single conversations. We are only getting the highlight reel, and even that is woefully incomplete. The Gospels have almost nothing to say about the first thirty years of Jesus' life, and he apparently only lived three years after that. Abraham is seventy-five and then suddenly a hundred years old in the middle of the Genesis action. This is why the ancient Hebrews kept writing new books and commentaries (sometimes called "targums") on all this stuff for centuries, trying to fill in the gaps. We still are.

There are a few high points in the story: Abram gets rich, Abram meets the king of Salem, Abraham (eventually) has a son. But they are few and far between. Mostly, the narrative is about Abraham's waiting. It is pretty boring, like running in the wilderness. Even the visions get boring.

"After this," the text skips ahead in Genesis 15:1, into some indefinite future, having crossed some indefinite past. "The Word of the Lord came to Abram in a vision."

I know that a direct divine vision is meant to be a big deal, but if I'm Abram, I will wake right up the moment the vision starts and start screaming at the walls. I will shout a lecture at the sky. If I'm Abram, I'm sick of being promised things, sick of being told I am chosen, sick of being complimented. I've had the visions and built the stupid monuments. I don't need another divine "attaboy."

2. Stevens, *The Marathon Monks of Mount Hiei*, 133.

But Abram doesn't wake up to protest and so the vision unfurls. It is the same old stuff but more ironic, like a dagger to the heart. God begins in the form of a Hebrew poem.

"Do not be afraid, Abram." The first line in the stanza.

I can't help but wonder about Abram's interior response. "I'm not afraid. I'm tired. Tired of wandering around. I'm asleep, for God's sakes."

"I am your shield," the poetic morphism.

"I don't need a shield. No one is attacking me. I just finished routing the militias of four kings, and I never once asked for your protection."

"Your very great reward," and the poem ends.

"Yeah."

Even in the text, without my prognostication, Abram has had enough. "But Abram said, 'Sovereign Lord, what can you give me since I remain childless?" Enough of the encouragement already. Abram cuts to the chase.

And then, fire.

"He took him outside and said, 'Look up at the sky and count the stars . . . so shall your offspring be.'"

God had never used this luminous visual of the stars with Abram. There they are with the night sky, soaking in the promise. Abram's simple response would later become the very foundation of Paul's letter to the Romans, perhaps the most important treatise of Christian theology in existence. His response would become the foundation of Western Christianity. "Abram believed the Lord, and he credited it to him as righteousness."

Through his doubt, and cynicism, and frustration, he reups once again. It takes so little for God to smash in. "Ok, God, I believe." Or perhaps more literally, "I choose to believe."

E.W. Kenyon wrote, "Faith is acting in the face of contrary evidence."[3]

Most of my life, I have loved the sport of golf. When the kids came along, I stopped playing much, as little as once or twice per

3. Kenyon, *His Word is Now*, 16.

year, but that didn't bother me. It's enough for me to go to the driving range and just hit the ball to watch it soar. It is quiet and soothing and solitary. On TV, it is all these things mixed with individual grit and competition, like the running monks.

Professional golf is worlds apart from other sports because winning is almost infinitely elusive. Players routinely make millions of dollars without ever winning. Baseball players who earn less have to wear a disguise in public, but nobody knows these golfers from Adam. One played almost 400 PGA tournament events and earned an average of almost $40,000 per weekend, yet never won. That's how hard it is.

Imagine the rigor of the life of this sport: insanely long practice days, especially through the short off-season. For every tournament you enter, there is at least one day of practice rounds, then four days of tournament play. It is a constant bout with weather, with ailments, with loss. The best players in the world make catastrophic shots all the time. It reminds me of how the great Ta-Nehisi Coates characterized writing in an interview as an "entire process about failure."[4]

Most of them don't look much like athletes. These are journeymen who are in it for the craft, the everyday believers. And then maybe, once they have bled enough, fire.

Watching most pros win is as dramatic as an Italian opera. They can hardly believe it, all evidence to the contrary. It feels like luck, regardless of having put in years of the longest days of hard work. If you want to see a grown man cry, just watch the golf tournament on TV most Sundays. He is, in the best of terms, ecstatic.

I am convinced that in the solitude of the middle, we need such moments. We need ecstasy.

I love the banality of the beginning of Genesis 15 because it matches the banality of so much of the story. God reiterates the

---

4. Green, "Advice on Writing from *The Atlantic*'s Ta-Nehisi Coates," https://www.theatlantic.com/culture/archive/2013/09/advice-on-writing-from-i-the-atlantic-i-s-ta-nehisi-coates/465582/

promise to Abram for some reason. Abram complains. God says it again. Abram says, "Ok." God is impressed.

But then, once again, fire.

"So the Lord said to him, 'Bring me a heifer, a goat and a ram . . . ' Abram brought all these to him, cut them in two and arranged the halves opposite each other." Abram has made his altars to God and now God will reciprocate.

I think it's important to take a break in the action just to note that this part of the story, in terms of history, is pointless. Nothing new is offered. If it doesn't happen, it doesn't matter. We already know of the covenant, and circumcision is the one that will really matter to the Jewish people for millennia to come. Nothing happens here in material reality. Abram is old, worn out, and disappointed when the scene starts and old, worn out and disappointed when the scene ends. My point is that this is not for them, this is not for history, this is for Abram.

"When the sun had set and darkness had fallen, a smoking firepot with a blazing torch appeared and passed between the pieces. On that day the Lord made a covenant with Abram and said, 'To your descendants I give this land, from the Wadi of Egypt to the great river, the Euphrates.'"

It is said that the Bedouin people in this same region today still make such covenants, that they stand in the blood between halved animals to make ultimate vows to one another. It's wild to me that the covenant with Abram, which will soon get all of the biblical press, is the covenant of circumcision, but this is the first one. This is God entering Abram's banality with thunder, if but for a moment. This is ecstasy, straight from the source.

In 1623 somewhere in France, a mathematical prodigy was born to a tax accountant who would quickly be widowed. By the age of seven, Blaise Pascal was removed from school so that he could explore his own curiosities, which quickly came to center around mathematics. He completed dozens of Euclid's propositions without even being aware of them, and, eventually, Blaise Pascal grew to become the leading mathematician in France, publishing materials on "conic sections" at sixteen years of age, inventing a calculator at eighteen, moving on to a groundbreaking study of barometric pressure, etc.

And then, in the middle of all of this ascendancy, fire.

We don't really know what happened, some divine meeting like an Abrahamic experience, something profound. This is what he wrote:

> The year of grace 1654, Monday, 23 November.
>
> From about half past ten at night until about half past midnight, FIRE.
>
> GOD of Abraham, GOD of Isaac, GOD of Jacob not of the philosophers and of the learned. Certitude. Certitude. Feeling. Joy. Peace. GOD of Jesus Christ. My God and your God. Your GOD will be my God. Forgetfulness of the world and of everything, except GOD. He is only found by the ways taught in the Gospel. Grandeur of the human soul. Righteous Father, the world has not known you, but I have known you. Joy, joy, joy, tears of joy.[5]

After he died, the note was found sewn into the lining of his coat pocket. He kept it with him every day. He wore it on his person all those decades, this reckoning, his gospel of ecstasy.

I have had a few moments like this, and I am as dumbfounded by them as Pascal, so any speech would be slurred like his. The one that comes to mind was just minutes before performing water baptisms at a retreat, and I stepped out of the room alone, and there were visuals that God seemed to have arranged on the porch, and fire shot through me, and I felt some great love that seemed to threaten to smother me, to tear me asunder, to bring me home. And I could not shake the image, standing there, that the Lord, without having asked, was down on his knees in a towel, washing my feet.

I think that we have all had such moments if we are paying attention, which few of us probably are. But nonetheless, they are there. Annie Dillard calls them the gaps, "the altitudes and

---

5. Chappell, *Epiphanes*, 389.

latitudes so dazzlingly spare and clean that the spirit can discover itself for the first time like a once-blind man unbound." Her command? "Stalk the gaps."[6] The gaps are in those moments of sight, of unbounded yet bounded existence. The gaps are in the mountains and streams, the stars and the sacrifices. The gaps are in dreams and visions, in pleasures and pains, at the apex of a great cause. God isn't only in the gaps, of course, but ecstasy is, and we need it in the middle.

We don't get the gaps very often, but when you find one, sew the evidence into your clothes and don't let it go.

One of the desert monks in the fifth century, Abbot Joseph, was asked by a fellow Abbot what more he should do to please the heart of God. The legend says that he held his hands up, and each finger turned into a lamp of fire. He responded, his hands aglow, "Why not be changed into fire?"

---

6. Dillard, *Pilgrim at Tinker Creek*, 269.

8

Doubts: Doorways of the Middle

Now Sarai, Abram's wife, had borne him no children. But she had an Egyptian maidservant, named Hagar; so she said to Abram, "The Lord has kept me from having children. God, sleep with my maidservant; perhaps I can build a family through her." Abram agreed to what Sarai said.—Genesis 16:1–2

And your doubt may become a good quality if you train it. It must become knowing, it must become critical. Ask it, whenever it wants to spoil something for you, why something is ugly, demand proofs from it, test it, and you will find it perplexed and embarrassed perhaps, or perhaps rebellious. But don't give in, insist on arguments and act this way, watchful and consistent, every single time, and the day will arrive when from a destroyer it will become one of your best workers—perhaps the cleverest of all that are building at your life.—Ranier Maria Rilke, *Letters to a Young Poet*

AT ITS CORE, DISTANCE running is an ongoing argument within the self. Yes, there are those moments of natural symmetry where body, mind, and emotions are harmonized, but these are fleeting. Physiologically, you are generally at war with yourself. Your skin cells are telling your brain that you are overheating. Your big expensive brain is calculating what appears to be a waste of calories that it would rather have, urging you to stop. None of it is true. Your very cells are lying to you., your brain the saboteur. They haven't really evolved much since we were living in caves, running for our lives from the creatures. The cells still think everything is scarce, so they seek to withhold.

The science of all this changed a few decades ago with the popularity of ultra-marathons.

Most Americans can't run a mile, so the thought of a marathon feels as improbable as flapping your arms and flying. For centuries, the 26.2 miles of a marathon was seen as the ultimate challenge. And then it wasn't. Elite runners realized that there was no objective reason to stop. The theory goes that if you keep your calories balanced, stay hydrated, and maintain the proper form, you can just keep going. I've met people who are visibly overweight who run ultras. Hundred-mile races are now pretty pedestrian. Even longer races are held in the desert . . . in the summer. Dean Karnazes ran 350 miles in 81 hours without stopping to sleep so that he could beat the record of Pam Reed, who ran 300 miles in 80 hours. We humans sell ourselves short, we are so capable.

In reality, whether we are talking about one mile or 200, the key is to win the argument with yourself. Your doubts, though imprinted into your very cells by prehistoric biology and whatever version of logic we have inherited, are often inaccurate. They are important, but they are not telling you the things that are necessarily true. However, I believe that they can lead you toward truth if you follow their trail.

When my youngest daughter was eight years old, I asked her where she would like to visit if she could travel anywhere in the world. Her answer was forthright: "Monticello." My cup runneth over.

We flew into Richmond early on a Friday and then drove to the plantation. It is a land of shadows and ghosts; the property's mystique was exacerbated that morning by a sweltering fog. We toured the house and walked the grounds. Though I was well familiar with Thomas Jefferson, it was remarkable to see his genius through the objects that comprised his life: maps, fossils, journals, scientific tools, musical instruments, and the famous library. At the end of our visit, we began the slavery tour on Mulberry Row.

I was not prepared for the emotional impact of this final tour. It was not the reconstructed dirt floor shacks that got to me or the Hemmings saga, or even the reality that this President owned over 600 human beings during his lifetime. I knew those facts from books. What the facts can't make you feel is proximity. Mulberry Row is in the physical shadow of the mansion.

I simply could not shake the conception of people being born, living, and dying, knowing nothing beyond a few acres in the shadow of such opulence. They lived in a closed, totalitarian universe that defined reality. Those born there must have simply assumed that was the way the world had always worked: whites in the mansions, blacks in the shacks, world without end.

I walked to the President's grave, and when my daughter trailed off, I shook my fist. "Curse you," I said out loud. Being intrinsically patriotic, something seemed to die in me that day. It is a powerful moment of realization to look it all in the face, that the titan whom we have forever canonized was sleeping with his slaves. To lose a belief is to lose everything. Something that seemed so solid, now riddled with holes, prey to the shotgun blast of doubt.

There is always the tendency to want to help God.

I get it. The promise was slow in coming. God makes the promise, even dramatically seals it with a covenant years later in Genesis 15, but still, no baby. Imagine the waiting. Abram does nothing, but Sarai has had enough of that.

The funny thing about divine ends-around is that the reverse psychology required to help God fulfill his promise is actually based on the very fact that the promise came from God. Think about that. This is rather the nature of doubt. Sarai announces, "The Lord has kept me from having children." It's God's fault that he won't fulfill his own blessed word, which makes us angry, so we are going to help him in his poor impotence. But in the end, like

Adam and Eve walking out of the Garden of Eden forever, we still have to deal with God. Is there another option?

It is good to be angry with God and it is good to doubt. Anger and doubt make us take God seriously. The enslavement of the Israelites in Egypt is 400 years of anger and doubt. The book of Job is a forty-plus chapter tirade of anger and doubt. The cross of Christ is anger and doubt. And there is beauty in the midst of and even through all of these losses. The doubt seems like it leads us away from God, but in fact, it leads us toward him.

I mentioned Job because I love that it is in the Bible. Traditionally, Job was even thought to be the oldest story in history, predating Genesis. Think of it, the Bible's first book is largely about how the "arch of the moral universe bends toward" madness, and all we have to blame for this is God. The Bible's first book is about the sanctioning, even the hallowing, of doubt. In ancient Jewish interpretation, Job has been so pervasively connected to Abraham that one scholar invented the term, *Jobraham*, to reflect the marriage.[1]

The story is so famous that even the uninitiated have heard of "the patience of Job." In the opening chapters, God strikes a deal with the devil, and Job loses everything: property, wealth, health, children. His wife is spared, and her best advice for Job is to "curse God and die" (2:9). And you thought your morning traffic commute was purgatorial.

Apart from this narrative setup and epilogue, however, the Book of Job consists of a vast series of poems about God and the way he has ordered the universe, "an X-rated lament psalm," according to Richard Middleton.[2] There are accusations and a mountain of curses. Job is the central speaker, of course, but the microphone keeps being handed to an array of individual friends who have shown up to explain his situation. There are nuances in their approach, but they agree on one thing: This calamity must be

1. Ellis, "The Reception of the Jobraham Narratives in Jewish Thought," 124–40.

2. Middleton, *Abraham's Silence*, 81.

Job's fault because God is predictable. "As I have observed, those who plow evil and those who sow trouble reap it," one friend says (4:8). God rewards the righteous and smites the rest. The faithful in the mansions, sinners in the shacks, world without end.

But Job will not relent in his insistence that he has done nothing wrong. Job demands reasons, an audience with God. "I sign now my defense—let the Almighty answer me; let my accuser put his indictment in writing" (31:35). The end of the poem is like the heavyweight boxing title that Job has asked for. The intensity of the buildup is palpable. Job walks in one side of the arena, "Innocent," embroidered in bold letters across his boxing shorts. His opponent climbs into the ring on the opposite side, and the back of his robe reads "God." The fight is not pretty.

"Who is that darkens my counsel with words without knowledge? Brace yourself like a man; I will question you, and you shall answer me" (38:2). And question God does. He asks Job if he knows where the earth came from, if he has ever seen a dinosaur. God asks him if he knows how rain is made, or the purpose of winter. He asks if he has seen the mountain goats give birth, or grasps the aerodynamics of hawk flight. It is like that time when Mike Tyson knocked out Michael Spinx in ninety-one seconds. It is on first pass, "a rhetorical 'shock and awe' campaign meant to abase Job and put him in his place."[3] Job gets pummeled for a few chapters, then God reloads. "Will the one who contends with the Almighty correct him? Let him who accuses God answer him" (40:2). The last round is brutal, Job's ears both cauliflower. At last, his side throws in the towel. "Surely I spoke of things I did not understand," Job relents, "things too *wonderful* for me to know" (42:3).

"Wonderful," that's how Job summarizes God. "Life sucks, it's all your fault, and you're wonderful."

Middleton explains, "In other words, he has come to accept that the fragile nature of the human condition, with all its suffering (the human status as 'dust and ashes,' which he has experienced), is not incompatible with the royal dignity and importance of

3. Middleton, *Abraham's Silence*, 103.

humanity in God's sight, evident in God's willingness both to hear Job's complaint and to answer him."[4]

And in the end, when Job gets up off the mat, and his friends are reflecting on the statistics of the match, God directs the last spoken words in the book to Job's judges: "You have not spoken of me what is right, as my servant Job has."

God prefers reality to symmetry. God would rather talk about the beauty and terror of creation than pass out easy answers. God is big enough to be assaulted. God would rather us shake our fist than systematize. God prefers doubt.

> The book of Job thus suggests that between the extremes of blessing God explicitly (which is, of course, appropriate speech and which Job does at the outset) and cursing God (which is clearly folly, and which Job therefore avoids), there is the viable option of honest, forthright challenge to God in prayer, which God (as Creator) both wants and expect of those made in the divine image—and this is right speech too.[5]

Gregory of Nyssa wrote, "Concepts create idols. Only wonder understands." Doubt, it seems to me, is an open doorway to wonder.

My favorite doubters in biblical history are Jesus' own disciples, and not even when he is walking around doing miracles and talking cryptically about himself. I'm talking about when he is resurrected before them, in the flesh. In Matthew's telling, Jesus instructed them to meet him at a certain mountain, and there they met. Matthew 28:17 may be my favorite verse in the Bible. "When they saw him, they worshiped him; but some doubted." What's even better is that translators have largely assumed the contrast between the worshippers and the doubters, but the original language doesn't require that. It's a judgment call. We could equally read the ancient Greek text: "When they saw him, they worshiped and they doubted."

4. Middleton, *Abraham's Silence*, 125.

5. Middleton, *Abraham's Silence*, 128.

If there was ever a time for certainty, it would seem to be when the resurrected Jesus is standing in front of you, talking and glowing. But that's what's important about doubt. Its opposite is certainty. Its partner we call faith.

This is why Sarai and Abram's decision to take a shortcut is not just an act of doubt, but also an act of faith. And even though it might have been nearsighted, with unforeseen consequences, God gives the utilitarian heir the same promise of the miraculous one: "I will so increase your descendants that they will be too numerous to count" (16:10). God says of that great doubter, Job, that "he has spoken of me what is right" (42:8). Jesus sends his worshiping, doubting disciples to "make disciples of all nations." Doubt doesn't seem to bother God in the least bit. For heaven's sakes, he keeps choosing the doubters.

Frederick Buechner wrote, "Doubts are the ants in the pants of faith. They keep it awake and moving."[6] This is a beautiful line that depicts the interconnectedness between faith and doubt. At the beginning of life, the faith is enough and it will fuel you. Faith feels like certainty when you are young. In the end, I imagine that same faith to be like a featherbed you rest upon. But in the middle, you need the one to sustain the other. In the middle, sometimes the only voices that ultimately reveal the truth, are those that are lying to you.

6. Buechner, *Beyond Words*, 85.

9

Pain: Entering the Holy

"And every male in Abraham's household, including those born in his household or bought from a foreigner, was circumcised with him."—Genesis 17:27

"Strangely violent is the grace of gods who sit enthroned in holiness."—Agamemnon (4th century BCE)

ATHLETICS OF ANY SORT involves managing pain, but distance running is different. Running for hours is synonymous with pain. You inflict difficulty upon your physiology every time you lace up and get out. I saw a sign once at a distance race when I thought I was going to drop dead any second: "If it were easy I would do it."

Don't get me wrong, running isn't all pain. The endorphin boost of "runner's high" is a real thing. There are stretches of flow where it can be effortless and you feel like you can keep going forever. But those are stretches.

There is, of course, the pain of falling down, which is a staple of the sport. I once split my chin open while slowing down to take a break at an aid station. I've never seen a bone pop out, but I've seen some bad falls. Heck, I've jumped right over people who collapsed in front of me. Don't judge me, it's a competition.

Once I was hauling down a hill, just over three miles in, and a car was approaching. I moved over to the curb, jumped it with no problem. I saw an elevation in the sidewalk, didn't raise my right toe quite high enough, and sprawled out on the cement. I must have slid a foot and a half, road rash all over my shirt-less chest. Knees and elbows were all bleeding and I feared I had cracked my left knee. I stood there for a minute, shook it off, then ran nine more miles. When I got to work, I noticed that blood had soaked through my button-down shirt. I paid for it all day after, and it was worth every wince.

In the middle, pain is like childbirth. You have to seek it, it hurts, and it also gives you life.

Typically, the pain is not a centralized event like this, it's just a companion on the journey. I have found that it typically takes me forty to fifty minutes just to get comfortable. Sometimes the first five miles just feel hellacious, and then all is well. I read an interview with a professional runner who won the New York Marathon, and she essentially said no matter how physically and mentally prepared you are, you never know how you are going to feel on the day of the race. It might suck the whole time, but that doesn't mean you are doing something wrong. It doesn't mean you're not going to win.

I have learned to think about this pain as your ticket to the race, pain as entrance. The pain releases capabilities. The pain leads to the high. And as much as I don't like it, life and God seem to work the same way.

I have heard that the Hebrew sense of time is not linear, as we are accustomed to, but cyclical. Most of the Hebrew Bible seems to be devoted to this in Israel's relationship with God at large: Israel leaves the Lord for other gods, bad things happen, Israel cries out to the Lord, the Lord patches her up, then repeat the sequence every generation for half a millennium. It reminds me of Leo Tolstoy's famous line in Anna Karenina: "Each unhappy family is unhappy in its own way." You just wonder how the cycle never dawned on them, the capacity to make a different choice.

The Abraham story is similar but also horribly different. The cycle in Abraham's case is driven by God. It is hard to follow, impossible to systematize. I kind of chuckle at a whole branch of academia entitled "Systematic Theology." Walter Brueggemann says that God is

> ... irascible in freedom and pathos-filled in sovereignty, one who traffics in hiddenness. This God does not fit much of our theological preference and certainly does not conform to any of our bourgeois reductionism. This God is the one who keeps life ragged and open, who refuses domestication but who will not let our lives be domesticated either.[1]

Have fun with the business, professors, of systematizing the hurricane.

After Hagar has Abram's first child, which does virtually nothing to propel the story forward other than to highlight Sarai's feistiness, God is at it again. He already made a covenant with Abram years ago and in dramatic fashion. Now turn up the drama.

Thirteen years have passed since Ishmael was born, and in the text, it is like the so-called "silent period" between Malachi and Matthew. Nothing is happening, or at least nothing worth making it into the story. Just more trafficking in hiddenness.

I have often thought that the stories of Jesus' resurrection are so terrifying because He keeps showing up in the most ordinary of circumstances. The initial announcement in Matthew's gospel makes this a matter of geography: "He has risen from the dead and is going ahead of you into Galilee," back to the ordinariness, the familiar. The better show in my view would be for Jesus to march down the center of Jerusalem, his nail-scarred hands lifted high, Jesus Christ Superstar! But instead, he goes back to the dirt roads and forever fields, the quiet places, the living rooms, and the pots and pans. And you might be chatting with your friends in a living room or trying to catch some fish or walking on the road and suddenly he appears in the corner and he expects you to cook for him and then he wants to pronounce some things. He wants to show up out of nowhere and order everybody around for heaven's sakes. Anne Lamott once wrote that when she realized Jesus was

---

1. Brueggemann, "Counterscript," 27.

stalking her, strung out and addicted as she was, it felt like a black cat following her around. She kept searching her house for signs of an intruder. Who really wants this?

I don't mean to re-trod older ground, but here God goes again with Abram, re-trodding older ground. "When Abram was ninety-nine years old, the Lord appeared to him and said, 'I am God Almighty; walk before me and be blameless. I will confirm my covenant between me and you and will greatly increase your numbers.'" God is at it again, stirring the pot, dangling the ultimate and illusory prize yet again, breaking the poor old man's heart.

Much of what follows next is not surprising, because it is a recapitulation of all of the other promises God has made over the years, every time he has suddenly showed up in the corner out of nowhere and pronounced things to Abram. But this time, the covenant that God recapitulates with Abram is going to require action, a sign for all time. In order to accept the promise, Abram is going to have to cut his penis.

Who really wants this?

In ancient terms, it actually does make at least a modicum of sense. Survival itself depended on fertility, much less nation building. The penis was the fountain (apologies) of such fertility. God would create a people from Abram's fertility, so this organ shall be so marked. The very term, covenant, comes from the Hebrew word "to cut," and formal covenants typically included some sort of letting, like a blood oath.

Still, there is the pain. Abram laughs at first, the promise being more hilarious as the years have marched on. Then he sharpens the knife and does the deed, not only to himself but to Ishmael and all the other males in his caravan. And thus, one of the odder traits of Jewishness began, for no reason other than God makes a contract with His people. On God's side, He will sustain them. On their side, they will accept pain.

C.S. Lewis famously wrote, "God whispers to us in our pleasures, speaks in our conscience, but shouts in our pain: it is His megaphone to rouse a deaf world."[2]

2. Lewis, *The C.S. Lewis Signature Classics*, 604.

Pain is your ticket to the race.

The United States, though less than 5 percent of the global population, consumes over half of the world's medicines. We are in a veritable stupor as a people, numbed into nothingness by opioids, alcohol, incessant competition, screens. Our vigor and agency have been exchanged for painlessness. Pain for us is, in the words of J.K. Huysmans, "a useless, unjust, incomprehensible, inept abomination."[3] How did we get here?

I suppose we have to start with money, the omnipotent narcotic. The Industrial Revolution enabled us to have cheap things we couldn't have before. We won World War II and became a superpower. Our individualism and initiative led to boundless entrepreneurial creativity. We suddenly had both disposable income and leisure time, a mostly new phenomenon in the history of civilizations. The profit motive wrapped all this up with a bow and filled in all the gaps with its boring sludge.

Now we live in what Christopher Hedges calls an "empire of illusion," and that illusion is a world full of quick fixes to pain. As if the point of pain is to be fixed. Lawyers advertise cheap divorce on billboards: $499 uncontested! Credit cards provide for immediate wants, no need to dither with the pain of delayed gratification. One of my favorite headlines in the satirical newspaper, The Onion, simply reads: "New Remote Control can be Operated by Remote." We sit on the couch, alone, indebted, rich, and ingloriously pain-free.

And in this silenced state, we should indeed be terrified of the prospect of God appearing in the corner because you can bet that if he does, He's bearing a sharpened knife, a cross, and He means to use it.

One of the most popularized stories of Jesus, even in the present secular zeitgeist, was his propensity to heal lepers. In ancient Jewish communities, as prescribed in the Torah, people with such infectious skin diseases were ostracized, disallowed from living in towns or villages. The crowds undoubtedly parted if one were to

3. Huysmans, *Against the Grain*, 128.

walk by. Jesus not only heals them, he touches them to heal them as if to pick a fight with their caste system. His purity is transferable.

For centuries, it was assumed that such persons had a flesh-eating bacteria of some sort, but a few decades ago, that was disproven. Leprosy, which still exists today, is a disease of the nerve endings. When nerve endings suddenly turn off, the patient can no longer feel. They go blind because the eyelids no longer feel the need to blink. Small injuries go unheeded and therefore get infected. Things are falling apart, and the afflicted does not even know.

What this means is that, medically speaking, when Jesus touches and thus heals the leper, the touch is a dagger. Jesus is giving the leper back the gift of pain.

No one is born with leprosy. It is contracted later in life. Numbness is the business of the middle, you see. And circumcision, pain, is the only way out.

"I will show him how much he must suffer for my name," Jesus says to Paul, calling him from the vigor of youthfulness to the pain of the middle. "When you are old you will stretch out your hands, and someone else will dress you and lead you where you do not want to go," Jesus says to Peter in their final conversation, indicating the horror of his future death. To disciples on a road to Emmaus who failed to recognize him, Jesus was incredulous. "Did not the Christ have to suffer these things and then enter his glory?"

How is it that we expect a different path?

An ancient rabbi in the Mishnah says, "Great is circumcision, for despite all the commandments which Abraham our father carried out, he was called complete and whole only when he had circumcised himself." A different rabbi, commenting right beneath this says, "Great is circumcision, for if it were not for that, the Holy One, blessed be he, would not have created his world."

10

Laughter: Holy Irreverence

Then the Lord said to Abraham, "Why did Sarah laugh and say, 'Will I really have a child, now that I am old?' Is anything too hard for the Lord? I will return to you at the appointed time next year and Sarah will have a son." Sarah was afraid, so she lied and said, "I did not laugh." But he said, "Yes, you did laugh."—Genesis 18:13–15

"They believed that the One who created time in its goodness and set the world afloat on it like a flowered barge is as ill-tempered and irrational and vengeful as one of their own kings. Yet they never ceased singing his praises even so, adjuring each other to love him with all their might when they had every reason in the world to hide from him in terror. It is no wonder that even in the Presence itself, I find myself shaking with laughter."— Frederick Buechner, *On the Road with the Archangel*

THEY ALWAYS SAID IT could never be done. But that is also just what they say. It was said about the four-minute mile, then came Roger Bannister in 1954, and now it is just another everyday benchmark. It was said about Roger Maris's home run record, and now he ranks eighth on the single-season list. It was said about a quarterback who was too old, and then Tom Brady won his seventh Super Bowl at forty-three. In my high school senior yearbook, I included a quote from some Proverb: "He who says it cannot be done should not interrupt the one who is doing it."

But distance running is different. It awakens the mind, soul, and body to limitations. Yes, the Olympians have incredible time splits, but no one can legitimately sprint at a dead heat for hours. This is why they also said that no one would ever complete a marathon in under two hours. And then came Eliud Kipchoge.

He didn't need another record to pad his resume. Kipchoge had been an Olympic champion and set the world record in Berlin in 2018 with a startling time of 2:01:39. The guy simply never lost. Other pros dodged races he entered that weren't even the big ones. He was thirty-six, not young, soft-spoken, and despite being fairly rich from his winnings, he lived on a farm in Kenya, growing his own food, and just running. But he always had his sights on the big enchilada.

He tried a two-hour marathon at a racetrack in 2017 but missed it by twenty-five seconds. Two years later, in Vienna, Austria, he tried again. To put it in perspective, he had to run over thirteen miles per hour to break the record, which is faster than the setting on every treadmill I have ever seen. If you have ever run a 5k, he clocked it at 14:10 . . . with 40k to go after that. In addition to the car that stayed in front of him, he had forty-two pace runners alongside, each taking their turns. Some were Olympians themselves, and it required forty-two of them to keep up such a blistering pace. He beat the two-hour mark by twenty seconds. "This shows the positivity of sport," he said when it was over. "Together when we run, we can make it a beautiful world."

My favorite thing about Kipchoge is that in every race, he smiles the whole time.

Back in 1978, a clinical psychologist named Daniel Levinson published a book about midlife that continues to have influence today. It was called *The Seasons of a Man's Life*, and Levinson described the male experience of middle age to be a journey through four distinct crises: being young vs. old, destructive vs. constructive, masculine vs. feminine, attached vs. separated. It sold a million copies. You have probably already caught onto the fact that it was Levinson who invented the concept of the midlife crisis.

We all know the stereotype well. Tom Cruise divorces Nicole Kidman for no real reason at all and next thing you know he is forty-two years old and jumping up and down on Oprah Winfrey's couch like a clown on the lunatic fringe, declaring his love for a young lady of twenty-six that he would also later divorce. I know someone who left his three children at forty-five to go shack up with some woman with two little girls, and now they live in a two-bedroom apartment with the girls. In fact, they predictably just bought a new sports car. If you live in the suburbs like me, you can tally up the number of midlife crises happening around you just by counting the Porsches in the driveways.

Here's what's funny though: the midlife crisis isn't quite a myth, but it is extraordinarily uncommon. Research shows that it's just not how midlife works for almost all of us. The year after Levinson's book came out, a study at Harvard shredded it to pieces: "Just as pop psychologists have reveled in the not-so-common high drama of adolescent turmoil, just so the popular press, sensing good copy, has made all too much of the midlife crisis."[1] The statistic is something like 3 percent of men will experience some form of the crisis. It just makes for good movies and talk shows, acted out by crazed celebrities.

The real experience of midlife is far blander. The top three challenges? Physical changes, increased responsibility for others, and financial burdens. The truth of it is that life in the middle is beer guts and bills, not mistresses and Maseratis. We don't trample the couch, we just sit on it, straight-faced. We become so serious in the middle.

I think it is important to pause and remember where we are in the Abraham story. These ancient narratives are thick, and you can lose your sense of place. Abram is not the young man he was when called to leave his homeland; he has lived some years and is in the middle. There have been wars and drama and an

1. Vaillant, *Adaptation to Life*, 222.

illegitimate child and the outlandish promises too, but still no promise fulfillment in sight. And even though the story is still something of a Greek tragedy at this point, the promise still looms, and the big picture is massive.

The whole notion of biblical faith, the whole metanarrative, depends on this middle-aged couple and the promise they hold dear. It is a promise that they do not understand. First there is the promise that through Abram will come blessing and redemption to all the peoples of the earth, but what was that to them? Future legacy is of limited value when you are presently a walking pile of shame. The promise would eventually become not just that of Judaism, but of Islam and Christianity, who each claim to fulfill the blessing to the world. There is, wrapped into this promise to Abraham and Sarah, the entire biblical narrative, the work of God in history, the salvation of creation. It is all hinging on this promise of a child to them, and this promise alone. And this great promise begins with uncontrollable laughter.

Why did they laugh at the promise of a child this time? We do not know. God had told them the same thing plenty of times before, including in the preceding scene of the covenant. I guess it was the three mysterious visitors whom the text interchanges with God without commentary (in one ancient interpretation, Abram excuses himself from God so as to extend hospitality to the visitors, demonstrating the confusion of this interchange). It is unclear whether Abram understands them to be God or not. In interpreting this passage, the ancient rabbis tended to bypass that question and instead praise him for his immediate and passionate hospitality to strangers. The strangers tell Abram to get the nursery ready, and that is where the fun begins. It is where the gospel begins.

The story of the salvation of the world begins with the woman laughing. In the chapter before, Abram laughed so hard at the promise that he fell on his face, the first instance of laughter in the Bible, and now it is Sarai's turn. She fights it tooth and nail, for she knows its irreverence. Abram had been so respectable that he wouldn't even eat with his guests, and now she will laugh in their faces. She tries to hold it in but that just makes her choke. It explodes out of her like the wind, teeth, and wheeze. She shakes it all out, like a Pentecostal evangelist.

I just love that it is Sarah's laughter that is at the center of the story, and it gets better. God won't let her off the hook. The angel intervenes and asks about Sarah's laughter, and Sarai is scared stiff and denies the whole thing. Then God says, "No, you did laugh." And perhaps the wildest thing about it all is that, far from getting angry at them for laughing, in chapter 21, Abram and Sarai obey God's command to name the child Isaac, which means laughter. God wanted to make the biggest point he could, throughout all time, that the fulfillment of his promise to rescue all of creation through the birth of the nation through the child, Isaac, all started with laughter.

When I lived in Chicago, I took the rush hour train straight into Union Station, the heart of the financial district, then took the bus or walked another mile to the subway. There were people bustling everywhere, men in suits, women in dresses, on their way to trade stocks, or run hedge funds or manage the business of the law. They held onto their coffee and ignored the panhandlers. I was on my way to school in a doctoral program in my twenties, free as a bird, wearing jeans or shorts, inviting the homeless guys to breakfast sometimes. And I remember wondering why everyone on the street was so unbearably serious every day, the boring sameness of it all. I can see why Neil DeGrasse Tyson says that there is a reasonable possibility that we are actually living in a computer simulation.

Now, of course, I have joined their ranks, full of self-importance and shouldering all of these middle-aged responsibilities. Much of the time, I feel a bit glum, a low-grade stress being the new baseline. If the heart monitor could both spell and beep, it would read "b-o-r-i-n-g." My kids are teenagers, cars are a few months away, and college a few years. We are financially fine but I do have to work another few decades and you never know when the economy will crash next. A mid-life crisis would be much sparkier but this is where things are.

And Sarai tells us that in the middle, what we need is laughter.

Maya Angelou told the story about certain slave plantations in the American South where laughter was forbidden. The masters were nervous about the slaves laughing at them, nervous that this could start the whole system crumbling. So the slaves invented something. If they couldn't hold it in, they would tip themselves all the way down in a designated barrel, like they were searching for something on the bottom, and they would just roar it all out until they were done. They called it the laughter barrel.

I can envision them set out on the streets of Chicago for the businessmen and women, feet in designer shoes shaking up in the air. I can see them by the computer where we keep the bills, by the desks where we do our work, in the backseat of the car where we sit in traffic. It is something, this universal language. When we laugh, we claim the promise, whether we realize it or not.

There is a story in the Talmud about three famous rabbis who visit the destroyed temple after the Romans sacked Jerusalem. When they come upon its ruins, they see animals in the holy of holies. Two of them weep, but the greatest one, Akiba, laughs. He knows that, ultimately, God will have the last laugh. The two others responded, "Akiba, you have consoled us!"

11

Individuation: Scrapping in the Middle

"May the Lord not be angry, but let me speak just once more."—Genesis 18:32

"If I am not for myself, who will be for me? And if not now, when?"—Rabbi Hillel (1st Century CE)

SEVERAL YEARS AGO, I came up with some work projects out in Phoenix, Arizona. Anything I assumed about the Southwest I got from Western movies like *Tombstone*, so I didn't much know what to expect. Now I find excuses to go a few times per year. I am in love with it all: the desert, the climate, the endless, joyous trail running.

If I could start at the plane runway, I would just leave my bags behind. I go running before I check into the hotel. I have a bunch of routes now, but you can pull over most anywhere and hit trails. I like to find the mountain ridges with vast valleys on either side. You have to be careful about getting lost or falling off a cliff. You can go for hours without ever seeing another soul. There are moments of lostness where you just expect you might run up on Wyatt Earp and Doc Holiday, playing poker around a campfire. There is even a smell to the desert, like cherrywood. I know I'm going on and on, but it is just intoxicating.

There is also something about the desert that constructs the very ethos of the West which I find so attractive. The desert in the Southwest is boundless, unregulated, wild and punishing. Running in the desert feels untamed. I almost ran all night long once, caught up in it all.

One glimpse of those mountain trails and I want to disappear. I want to cheat at a poker game and see what happens. I want to sling a six-shooter off of my hip. I want to kill a diamondback with my bare hands. I want to walk into a bar and pick a fight. "Say when."

It is a good thing to still feel this virility in the middle, ridiculous as it is. I fear that if it ever runs out, the next step is death.

I have been reading what all sorts of ancient Jews wrote about Abraham. The living tradition of the Hebrew Bible is unspeakably vibrant. The Bible is just the base text for countless stories, additions, interpretations, and sermons called the *midrashim*. You might expect this material to cohere around the covenant God made, or the birth of Isaac, or circumcision. There is plenty on all that, but the rabbis had a particular favorite that is quite surprising: they love that Abraham bargains God down, attempting, albeit unsuccessfully, to talk God off the ledge of destroying Sodom and Gomorrah.

This is strange for a host of reasons, not the least of which is that Sodom and Gomorrah were, for all reasonable intents and purposes, hellholes. The Lord himself declares the same, that sin of these cities is "so grievous that I will go down and see if what they have done is as bad as the outcry that has reached me" (18:20–21). Our modernistic version of God as some abstract CEO of the cosmos is so unbiblical. In the Bible, God is constantly coming down here to check things out for himself, to get His hands dirty, and to be involved. He is an active agent in the world.

What God finds in the next chapter is like a Monty Python scene gone dark. Two of God's angels arrive as guests in the city. Whatever Abram's nephew, Lot, recognizes about them we don't know, but as we have already said, this was a culture in which heaven and hell bent to the standards of hospitality. Lot takes them in, feeds them, then the men of the town, in a gross affront to these ancient near eastern hospitality standards, demand to rape them. Lot horribly offers his daughters, thickening the tragedy, but that is not enough. Lot gets the word out: Vesuvius is about to blow. And so it was.

But before this divine scouting tour, none of this was a foregone conclusion. In fact, God tells Abram about the plan to destroy the cities, and Abram is sanctimonious. "Far be it from you to do such a thing—to kill the righteous with the wicked, treating the righteous and the wicked alike. Far it be it from you!"

We are so timid in our prayers; so pious. Back in my young days as a student at a Christian college, such precious gentleness led to the inarguably perfect breakup line: "God told me that we should no longer be together." Well, that rather buttoned up the matter. Who am I to argue with God?

Yet Abram thinks he is just the one to face off, calling God on the carpet, bidding him down six times, from fifty to ten. If God can find just ten righteous people in the town, the execution is stayed. And he is venerated and truly loved for this in Jewish tradition. Elie Wiesel contrasts the rabbis' celebration of Abraham with their alternate denigration of Noah:

> Did Noah do the same? Did he ever argue with God as Abraham did? Did he ever implore Him to show mercy? Did he ever utter a single word of protest—or prayer? Did he ever try to intercede with God on behalf of the countless human beings who were already doomed but didn't know it? As soon as he learned that he himself was not in danger, he stopped asking questions, he stopped worrying altogether . . . It was God who had to incite him to respond with anger.[1]

It is just so quintessentially Jewish, so brazenly biblical. God thinks all of our cowering is worth precisely zilch. Argue, scrap, make your case, stand up for things that matter, *be human* for

1. Wiesel, *Sages and Dreamers*, 27–28.

God's sakes. Virility is your ticket to divine respect, which is not unassociated with self-respect.

In the Mishnah, the rabbis are having another debate about arcane things, this time whether separate tiles could be used in an oven to cook proper kosher food. The sages before him disallowed this, declaring it unclean, but the great Rabbi Eliezer disagrees. The Sanhedrin cites the Torah's clear directive for multiple witnesses as a requirement for truth, and Eleazar is clearly out on his own. In fact, he is excommunicated from the group, case closed.

Until suddenly a voice from heaven cries out: "Why do you dispute with Rabbi Eliezer, seeing that in all matters the *hallacha*—the Jewish body of traditions—agrees with him?" One rabbi says the voice is from the devil, not from heaven. Another claims that the voice doesn't matter, for the Torah has already spoken. The text says that God's response was to roar with laughter. "My sons have defeated me," God twice announces.

Another passage in the Mishnah says that when all things are restored, God will take his place among the rabbis, and they will debate the proper interpretation of the Torah with its author, the Almighty.

I started taking classes in a professional mental health counseling program because I missed school and I have come to realize how little I process, much less comprehend about myself. I encountered Carl Jung, one of Sigmund Freud's colleagues, and a concept he called individuation.

Jung believed in an inherited collective unconscious, full of myths, archetypes, beliefs, symbols, and images that enable us to comprehend and navigate the world around us. The journey of maturity for Jung requires the ability to become conscious of almost anything, the challenge to discover "the unconscious aspects of our perception of reality."[2] The mechanism to achieve this is individuation, where we become separated from the collective

2. Jung, *Man and His Symbols*, 4.

unconscious so that we retrieve our own before then assimilating all of these parts into an integrated reality.

Easier said than done.

Individuation is seemingly easy in adolescence and young adulthood. The very nature of those life stages is this impetus to project uniqueness, to contribute to things in fresh, new, particular ways. A sense of identity is wrapped up in this flooring the gas pedal toward whatever you happen to be pursuing. There is so much newness.

But in the middle, you can so easily fall backward into the soft soup of the collective unconscious, where things seem old and comfortable and assumed. You cannot even imagine this when you are young, but it happens. You know that you are profoundly unoriginal in your thinking, your boring problems, your staid habits. You know how things work, world without end. You give into natural laws and the natural order of things. There is a certain lazy symmetry to it, and eventually, you can start to feel meaningless and meaninglessness altogether.

Abraham probably knows exactly what this is like. He is ninety years old now. He is not young anymore. He has catalogued a few dramatic moments through the years, but mostly not. He has mostly been walking and waiting on the promise, even just signs of the promise. By this point, he must know how things work. God will show up every now and then. God will have his way. In Abraham's context, the gods did what they wanted. Most of the creation myths that come from this time period and region envision humans to be slaves of the gods, there to build them temples and feed them with sacrifices. Abraham likely would have been glad to feel like such a divine pawn. Instead, he felt mostly duped and bored.

That, to me, is the beauty of Abram's bargaining with God: that it requires disassociating from the ancient near eastern collective consciousness, from everything he has ever known. In fact, there is actually no bargaining here; there is harassment. This is individuation, those moments of standing up, of untamed and sometimes even illogical agency that prevent us from drifting away into meaninglessness.

We have to be able to do both, to absorb the collective soup, to accept reality. Until we don't. There is also standing apart from it, which is the only way we make peace with it. There is a lovely Yiddish word for this posture: *chutzpah.*

At the ancient temple of Apollo in Delphi, "Know Thyself" was carved right onto the top. Is this what the God of Abraham is getting at, that if you are going to do business with me, you better be able to filter some things? You better be able to assimilate, yet stand apart. Jacob wrestles with God all night long and the result is a name-change and a blessing. The result is the beginning of Israel. God likes a good fight, so you better be able to disassociate from certain things. And you sure better be shored up to contend.

Sojourner Truth, born into slavery only to become perhaps the most famous female orator and abolitionist of the 19th century, was known for her white-hot faith and fervent prayers. When the cause was running out of funds, she cajoled God: "You know I have no money, but you can make the people do for me, and you must make the people do for me. I will never give you peace till you do!" Unsurprisingly, her most renowned speech, among the greatest in American history, was called, "Ain't I a Woman?" a raucous and (somehow) extemporaneous romp. She was, simply put, a paragon of dogged irreverence. Toward the end of her life, she said, "Though it seems curious, I do not remember ever asking for anything but what I got it. And I always received it as an answer to my prayers."[3]

3. Reagon, *If You Don't Go, Don't Hinder Me*, 121.

12

Loss: The Trail to Newness

"Then the Lord rained down burning sulfur on Sodom and Gomorrah—from the Lord out of the heavens. Thus he overthrew those cities and the entire plain, including all those living in the cities—and also the vegetation in the land."—Genesis 19:24–25

"There is a time in life when you expect the world to be always full of new things. And then comes a day when you realize that is not how it will be at all. You see that life will become a thing made of holes. Absences. Losses. Things that were there and are no longer. And you realize, too, that you have to grow around and between the gaps, though you can put your hand out to where things were and feel that tense, shining dullness of the space where the memories are."—Helen MacDonald, *H is for Hawk*

ALTHOUGH I DON'T IMAGINE that the Greeks alone invented official races, it is the famous contests at Olympia that made their indelible mark on the psyche of history, both Western and Eastern. Performed nude and before a male-only audience, the winner received fame, the coveted laurel wreath (what we often consider a "crown" in our translations), and even financial gifts from admirers. The short sprints were the most popular races, but there was a range of options, such as one that involved running in full armor. There were coaches, training programs, and even musicians who provided a certain rhythm for the runners. The Greeks considered running to be both scientific and philosophical, but even more importantly, running was to them the domain of the gods.

An ancient writer preserves a prayer from a young athlete, offered to the Greek goddess, Athena:

> Athena, Queen of the Aegis, by whatever name thou lovest best, give ear.
>
> Inasmuch as thou dids't heed my vow, and grant me fair glory at Mantinea, bear witness I have been not ungrateful. I have offered to thee a white sheep, spotless and undefiled. And now I have it in my mind to attempt the pentathlon at the next Isthmia at Corinth. Grant me victory even in that; and not one sheep but five, all as good as this today, shall smoke upon thine altar. Grant also unto me, my kinsmen and all my friends, health, riches and fair renown.
>
> And oh! gracious, sovran Athena, blast my enemy Xenon, who strove to trip me foully in the foot race. May his wife be childless or bear him only monsters; may his whole house perish; may all his wealth take flight; may his friends forsake him; may war soon cut him off, or may he die amid impoverished, dishonored old age. If this my sacrifice has found favor in thy sight, may all these evils come upon him unceasingly. And so will I adore the and sacrifice unto thee all my life.[1]

I told you that back then running was serious business. Such is our genetic fear, rooted in ancient times, of loss.

During the Covid-19 pandemic, I experienced the strangest theological shift, a discovery. I found the oddest solace and comfort in the prospect of the wrath of God. I knew that for God to resemble anything helpful required opposition to certain things, but it was harder to know what to do with that, how to pin it all down. I heard a Jewish rabbi say something to the effect that "God has sent the pandemic to end our consumerism . . . " and

---

1. Davis, *A Day In Old Athens*, 284.

even though I don't believe that, I wish I believed it, and I would be better off for believing it. It seems to me that a pretty good summary of the Bible is simply that it is better to contend with God than with chaos, or with nothing at all.

Abraham bargained with God, and it was all for naught. Humankind has always feared the terror of divine judgment. One Jewish legend said of Sodom and Gomorrah that "the sinful inhabitants of the cities of the plain not only lost their life in this world, but also their share in the future world."[2] Nowadays, we have so domesticated God that we chalk a lot of things up to randomness or bad luck, but that is incommensurate with our species. If we had a more literal name for ourselves, like the anteaters do, we humans would be called meaning-makers. And what is the meaning of the destruction of Sodom and Gomorrah? The meaning is loss.

I'm convinced that it is easy to focus on the wrong thing here. The lion's share of the passage is actually devoted to Abraham's nephew, Lot, and his unfortunate situation as a resident in the doomed region. Interpreters from ancient times to today have argued over exactly why God sacked the place, hence the transformation of the name, sodomy, in English. But the passage doesn't afford a clear answer because that isn't the point. "Early the next morning Abraham got up and returned to the place where he had stood before the Lord," even as he gazed over the smolder of the cities in the distance. That is the apex of the story.

Abraham goes back to the very spot where he had attempted to talk God off the ledge, and from there, he watched the cities burn. The very grass is burning, a wasteland. In the first century, the sophisticated Jewish writer Philo asserted that "to this day it goes on burning . . . providing proof of the sentence decreed by the divine judgment."[3] Abraham returned to the place where he tried with all of his wits to head off the catastrophe and there he contemplates what has been lost.

2. Ginzberg, *The Legends of the Jews*, 81.
3. Kugel, *The Bible As It Was*, 192.

It would be good for the soul, from time to time, to go to church and sing a worship song together about God's wrath, and all that it might take from us, and all that it might give.

When I was in middle school, Mike Tyson was on his tear to break every record that heavyweight boxing had ever seen. He was the youngest heavyweight champion ever, with a blistering start to his professional career that began at eighteen years old. He won thirty-seven straight fights, a slew of them in the first round. Michael Spinks was also undefeated; Tyson knocked him out in ninety-one seconds. Spinks was paid $13.5 million.

He really was awe-inspiring, the raw power and speed. He could barely string a coherent sentence together and it didn't matter (on his tour of Japan, he remarked, "They don't even speak English!"). People who never thought about boxing were suddenly glued to every fight. It was a frenzy, a Super Bowl each time he got into the ring.

I was regaling Tyson's invincibility to my Dad after the Spinks fight, and I'll never forget his response. "Eventually, Mike Tyson will lose," he said casually. My jaw dropped. I could not fathom such an event.

Then, in a fight billed "Tyson is Back!" by the promoters, Iron Mike met his 42:1 underdog in the Tokyo Dome. Analysts expected another ninety-second annihilation (Tyson had won the fight before in ninety-three seconds). Buster Douglas was considered a warmup match for Tyson. Tyson's cornermen didn't even bring ice. What's more, Douglas had the flu. Tyson partied with Bobby Brown the night before, calling Douglas "an amateur."

On February 11, 1990, Buster Douglas and Mike Tyson came reasonably close to killing each other. In the tenth round, Tyson suffered his first knockout. In fact, it was the first time he had even been knocked *down* in his professional career. Douglas wept during his interview after the fight and said it was all "because of my mother."

Douglas lost his next fight after Tyson and retired. Tyson never regained the title of heavyweight champion even though he went to jail and then fought on. These losses were the mid-point. The great rock band, The Killers, wrote a song about it ("Tyson vs. Douglas"), enshrining loss as art and meaning.

Did you know that humans are the only species who cry?

A few years ago, I had the opportunity to visit Chichen Itza, the great Mayan capital on the Yucatan Peninsula. It is known for its vaulted pyramid, but the ball stadium has stood for a thousand years as well. In the Mayan games, the losers got nothing. The winners were sacrificed to the gods.

This seems backward to us, but why must it be? The psychoanalyst Arno Gruen contends that "the actual sources of our cruelty and callousness lies in the rejection of our suffering."[4]

In a memoir that placed as a finalist for the Pulitzer Prize, Dr. Paul Kalanithi details his life as a poet brain surgeon, then the brain tumor that would quickly end his life. After his passing, his wife wrote a summation:

> Relying on his own strength and the support of his family and community, Paul faced each stage of his illness with grace—not with bravado or a misguided faith that he would "overcome" or "beat" cancer but with an authenticity that allowed him to grieve the loss of the future he had planned and forge a new one. He cried on the day he was diagnosed. He cried while looking at a drawing we kept on the bathroom mirror that said, "I want to spend all the rest of my days here with you." He cried on his last day in the operating room. He let himself be open and vulnerable, let himself be comforted. Even while terminally ill, Paul was fully alive; despite physical collapse, he remained vigorous, open, full of hope not for an unlikely cure but for days that were full of purpose and meaning.[5]

There is no resurrection without crucifixion, no new anything without loss. Look the loss in the eye. Go back to the spot

---

4. Gruen, *The Betrayal of the Self*, 281.
5. Kalanithi, *When Breath Becomes Air*, 219.

where you bargained with God and lost. Accept it. You may need to embrace it. "Cast your bread upon the waters," Ecclesiastes says, "and in many days it will return to you." But it cannot be the same bread that returns. Argue though you must, the raining fire and sulfur must come, the tenth-round knockout.

13

Grace: Reality in the Middle

"Then Abimelech brought sheep and cattle and male and female slaves and gave them to Abraham, and he returned Sarah his wife to him."—Genesis 20:14

"You cannot conceive, nor can I, of the appalling strangeness of the mercy of God." —Graham Greene, *Brighton Rock*

IN 1992, THE BRITISH runner, Derek Redmond, had set the world record for the 400-meter sprint . . . twice. He arrived at the Olympics in Barcelona that year true to form, winning his first race outright, then the second. He was poised to win the semifinal, when almost halfway through the race, the unthinkable happened. Like a rubber band stretched too far, his hamstring popped apart in an instant, and he crumpled to the ground.

A collective grasp tore through the crowd. This was rare at this level of competition, so rare that there was a pause as the finishers crossed the line and no one seemed to know what to do. Finally, there appeared to be a tussle with security in the stands. A large figure was bounding down the seats. No one knew what to make of it when he eluded security, then climbed over the wall onto the track.

It was Redmond's father. He put his arms around his son and they hobbled to the finish line, the crowd on their feet in a frenzy.

It remains one of the most remarkable moments not just in running, but in sports history.

Sometimes you are lying dead on your face in the middle of your failure, and grace happens.

I wonder at what point in life we tend to fall into predictability and routine. I doubt it has ever been said of a teenager, "She's so set in her ways!" Even young adulthood is a nonstop set of options. I remember once in college being woken up by friends in the middle of a Tuesday nap, and thirty minutes later, I was cutting class to jump off of a high cliff into a frigid river. The first decades of our lives are like this.

I suppose it's making a living for yourself that changes this dynamic. Even if you are a professional athlete or have an exciting job where you may travel and the scenery regularly changes, eventually it becomes a routine. None other than Lebron James does more or less the same thing every day, seven days a week.

Routines aren't bad, but they certainly aren't neutral. It is a good routine to pay your rent and utilities on time. It is a bad routine to smoke two packs a day. But what's more important is an awareness that in the middle, routines are really hard to break, and the bad ones virtually need steel bolt cutters.

After Abraham impressively barters God down even though in the end his math was wrong, Sodom and Gomorrah are famously destroyed, then . . . sameness. "Now Abraham moved on from there into the region of the Negev and lived between Kadesh and Shur." Abraham, that walking man, always falling back to living in between.

And then the story goes back to the start. You'd think that all of these dramatic experiences, these divine thin places that Abraham has visited would have fundamentally changed his character. But they didn't. The same boldness that Abraham exercised in the attempt to save two sorry cities is nowhere to be found when, once again, he fears the king of the town. He pawns off Sarah as his sister, as he did way back in Egypt. He should have learned the first time that this decision is stupid and has real consequences.

We find out in the last verse of the chapter that God put the kibosh on childbirth in the king's household "because of Abraham's wife Sarah." But routines are routines.

You might expect God to put his foot down, or at least a long divine eye roll. You might expect God to just move on, to find someone of greater pedigree and certainly loftier character. But what's wild is that God himself instead goes directly into cleanup mode. He is really the central figure in this story.

God visits the king in a dream, tells him what's up, that it's not his fault, that he needs to give Sarah back. God also calls Abraham a prophet in the dream, which is the only time this term is applied to Abraham and also its first occurrence in the Bible. What an odd moment to knight the old codger with such a grand title! Abraham, the pimping prophet.

The king is understandably not happy. He asks for a logic model, and Abraham draws it out, defending himself. Just like God, you would expect the king to throw Abraham out on the street. Instead, the illogic of grace scrambles all that is reasonable.

"I am giving your brother a thousand shekels of silver," the king tells Sarah, "to cover the offense against you." To Abraham, he gives livestock, slaves, and protection in the best of his land. It is breathtakingly lavish and unnecessary. It is like a parable, the sucker punch at the end. It is grace.

Finally, Abraham seems to get the point that grace is the antidote to fear. "Then Abraham prayed to God, and God healed Abimelech, his wife, and his slave girls so they could have children again." Grace begets grace begets grace.

I think a good bit these days about reality, what it is. Back in a doctoral program, I did a bunch of work on this, the anthropological models for how we humans construct reality. It sounds heady, but it's actually pretty straightforward.

Turns out there are three big schools of thought about reality. The structural-functionalist approach to reality is like a system that is attempting to keep itself balanced, like The Matrix. Reality is sort of like an equation, extremes being rounded out over time to keep the system in check. The conflict theorists see the opposite; reality is chaos that we do our best to navigate by getting whatever piece of the pie we can (it is interesting that a purely scientific view of nontheistic evolution fits into this view). The symbolic theorists see reality as our projection, the meanings that we have made that are attributed to everything. Thinking through this makes you realize that reality is really comprised of how you understand certain rules or the absence of any.

One year for my birthday, my wife bought me Ken Burns' massive documentary series on the history of baseball. For someone who loves sports, history, and being alone, this was a superb gift. It took me eight months to watch the dozens of hours, and I was blessed.

The origins of baseball are virtually unknown, though volumes have been written about it. Some say it came from an old game called round ball, others from the British military, others from some cricket variance. Unsurprisingly, if we could visit the first leagues that started forming in the nineteenth century, we would hardly recognize the game they were playing. There was a pitcher, a batter, bases, but that's about where the similarities cease. A baserunner had to touch all the bases but could do so in any order. The hitter was out if the ball was caught on the bounce. There was no foul territory. The pitcher couldn't take either foot off of the ground when throwing. The description makes the game seem like pure chaos to us today for one simple reason: the rules were different.

I'm not convinced of a lot of things, but I am of this. Reality does have rules. Rules make reality, reality. But if we attempt to engage our lives based on the wrong rules, the result is chaos. We can literally live in such a way that is contrary to reality, like perpetually spitting into the wind.

This was Abraham's trap: try as he may, he kept living against reality. He tragically thought that the rules of reality, whatever might be said of them, were not in his favor. The king will kill me for my wife because that's just reality. I better get what's mine because that's just reality. Nothing is free; everything costs. I need to keep these secrets because reality demands it. That's life.

And are stories like this not in the Bible because certain ancient people were calling those metanarratives into question so many thousand years ago? In these simple stories, they were subverting the idea of a cold, dark, purposeless universe. You know what reality is, Abraham? Reality is that God is really on your side. Reality is that you're a *schlep* in the middle of a *schemozzle*, and in return for that, you are going to get a motherload of treasures. Reality is that this pay dirt is just a foretaste of what God is going to give to you. Because reality is gift, not conflict or system or symbol, but gift. Reality is generosity.

A few years ago now, I was leaving my house to go to work early in the morning, and I noticed an envelope on the doorstep with what looked like a child's handwriting on the outside that said "The Rice Family." I assumed it was a birthday invitation for my little girls from one of the children in the neighborhood, so without opening it I put it on the dining room table and went to work. My wife messaged me a few hours later. "Why is there an envelope addressed to our family with seven hundred dollar bills in it and no note?" To this day I have no idea. It might be a purposeful story if we were about to lose our house or have the gas shut off but that is not the case. We had no urgent need for $700. The money sat in my desk drawer for months. It felt like blood money, like some sort of Abrahamic test from God. I never did bring myself to spend it, because I did nothing to earn it.

We are so uncomfortable with gift, with grace. We are uncomfortable with reality. Reality is that I have earned nothing. Every good thing in my life has been mysteriously dropped off, addressed to me by a God so full of joy and trickery that he leaves stacks of riches on my front porch and disappears without a trace.

A few weeks later, it happened again, more nameless cash, like a parable. A few months after that, it happened again, now totaling thousands.

Richard Rohr says, "Remember, 'God' is just a word for reality—with a face."[1]

1. Rohr, *The Universal Christ*, 27.

14

Marriage: Rooting Out the Tumors

Sarah said, "God has brought me laughter, and everyone who hears about this will laugh with me. Who would have said to Abraham that Sarah would nurse children? Yet I have borne him a son in his old age." But Sarah saw that the son whom Hagar the Egyptian had borne to Abraham was mocking, and she said to Abraham, "Get rid of that slave woman and her son."—Genesis 21:6–7, 9–10

"So ancient is the desire of one another which is implanted in us, reuniting our original nature, making one of two and healing the state of man."—Plato

WHEN I WAS IN high school, I started running in the steamy summers after dark. I don't know what prompted me to do it, but I found it serene. I had no music and no real running shoes. I ran alone in the silence. When I got to college, I discovered I could get up to forty-five minutes on a treadmill. This seemed impressive to me, so I went out and started running for an hour at a time. I walked on the university cross-country team on this stated premise alone: "I can run for an hour." I learned to up my miles, but it was excruciating most of the time. Even cross-country races are about speed.

I kept it up for years, running an hour or so. In my late twenties, I trained for a half marathon. I was slow, but I caught the bug.

I started upping my miles, shifting my form, learning to eat and drink straight out of my pockets without missing a step. I began to understand that runner's high people talk about, then to chase it. I did not have to stop. It started to become effortless.

The fastest distance runner in the world, who I already mentioned, the only man to break the two-hour marathon, runs with a smile on his face. You can't even detect exertion; it looks more like meditation. How is this possible, this transition from pain to pleasure?

There is one man who has done more to promote the sport of ultramarathon running than anyone else. In fact, before Christopher McDougal wrote *Born to Run*, hardly anybody even knew this sport existed, much less was possible. McDougal spent years chasing down the world's top endurance runners around the world, studying the history and science of it all. He especially focused on a tribe of barefoot runners called the Tarahumara in Mexico, though there are similar cultures around the world. His conclusion is just what the title suggests, but in a literal sense. We are biologically built to be hunter-gatherers, covering miles of ground in packs every day, but we accidentally became farmers. Our spines never even adapted to this stationary work, which we all feel in our bones. We evolved to stay on the move, not to settle. The double entendre of "settle" says it all. In our cells, we are nomads. We are, quite literally, born to run. This is not just evidenced in our feet, our backs, our physiology. Running is hardwired into our brains.

There is a wildly popular bestseller that has sold ten million copies worldwide, which is nuts for a work of nonfiction. It's called, *Sapiens: A Brief History of Humankind*, written by a Jewish scholar at Hebrew University in Jerusalem. Before recounting the short but excitable history of our species, the writer is concerned with a fundamental question: Why did the *homo sapiens* survive to become what we now consider synonymous with human beings?

This equivalence was not a foregone conclusion, for we were not the sole original human family. In fact, there was a point at which the *homo sapiens* survived alongside the *Neanderthal*, the *homo erectus*, and other species of humans who either perished or who we replaced. The surprising component of our rise to prominence seems to run quite counter to determinism, materialism, and evolutionary biology. In short, our brains were bigger than the other humans; too big to be exact. They are incredibly expensive for the body to maintain, even more so for primitive peoples scrapping by, consuming a quarter of our energy while doing nothing more to enable us to hunt or farm than the smaller brains of the other humans. We were given no claws, no saber teeth, no swinging arms, no poison venom, no racing legs. We were given big, gangly, wasteful brains. It is as if we were only marginally constructed to survive, and principally constructed to do things that have nothing to do with survival, like composing poetry and contemplating philosophy. Like falling in love. Annie Dillard writes, "We are one of those animals, the ones whose neocortexes swelled, who just happen to write encyclopedias and fly to the moon." Then, incredulously, "Can anyone believe this?"[1]

In the biblical tradition, the *homo sapiens* was special because this creature was given godlike responsibilities over the creation. Specifically, the species was imbued with the *image* of God, then charged with refracting and reflecting that image to the whole created order. I find it remarkable that with all of the shapes this reflecting of God's image could (and does) take, the first chapters of Genesis house the business of image bearing in a very specific, very familiar institution. In a time when there was a wide range of work to do in order to get the *homo sapiens* up off the ground, from farming, to hunting, to building a culture, the Creator locates the true manifestation of His image, the seedbed of true and full humanity, in plain old marriage.

"So God created man in his own image; in the image of God He created him; male and female he created them." The first poem in Genesis 1 crowns the fireworks of the creation story with the ultimate image of God discovered through man and wife. The second poem in Genesis 2 is so bent on making this point that it interrupts the narrative arch with a public service announcement: "Therefore a

1. Dillard, *For the Time Being*, 94.

man shall leave his father and mother and be joined to his wife, and they shall become one flesh," a verse that, according to the gospels, Jesus of Nazareth was fond of. The idyllic section of the creation poem ends with no reference to volcanoes, great white sharks, the aurora borealis. "If you want to see God's image," the poet seems to beckon, "don't sweat those physical wonders. God's image is right in front of you every day. It is sleeping right beside you at night." The crescendo of the poem concludes: "And they were both naked, the man and wife, and felt no shame."

That is the apex of the Bible's story of the origins of the *homo sapiens*. God gave us unnecessary brains, so that we might inefficiently love, even marry.

I am sitting at this moment in stone silence in a living room near Duke University with Nathan Artt, a man who has been a friend to me when I have needed a friend, one of those Doc Holidays that God drops in your lap a few times during your life if you are lucky. In the adjoining room, his young wife Jessica lies in a state that is sort of like sleep. Two days ago, her skull was opened and a large tumor resected.

The surgery was done manually, by the leading expert in such maladies at Duke University. He has performed over five thousand brain surgeries in the course of his career. The procedure was infinitely complex, due to the fact that part of the tumor pressed against that segment of the brain that enables speech and fine motor skills. The slightest miscue, a few thousand cells in the wrong direction, and Jessica would be stripped of her adulthood. She would have to learn to speak English again, learn to use her hands and feet. She was awake the entire time, identifying barnyard animal flash cards so that the surgeon would know if he was dangerously touching healthy tissue. With his own hands, he lifted the entire mass, as a priest lifts up the host. *Hoc est corpus meum.* He navigated inside that big, unruly organ, and healed it.

Now, we watch and wait as the brain slowly regenerates.

We are presently in what I am affectionately calling the "Children of the Corn" phase. The patient is in a rather catatonic state, able to respond to yes/no questions but unable to phrase her own. She gets up from the bed and walks around without warning, standing erect and staring blankly. We will laugh about this later, but with the right soundtrack it feels like a horror movie. It is like a zombie wandering about in pajamas.

We are told that this is normal, that Easter will come. We are told that she will steadily emerge over the next week or so. The brain will automatically reconnect itself. Neurons will re-spark. Language will return. The stone will be rolled away and the brain will resurrect.

And even though this resurrection seems like the work of a God whose majesty dwarfs words to me, that is actually not where the creator of the brain is best showing off. Just like the creation story, with unspeakable miracles erupting all around, His image is on display in the ordinary. I am watching the Genesis poem unfold again in this rented house. I never dreamed I would say this, but I am watching God's image flood through my friend Nathan, like a prism.

I was privileged to officiate at the wedding of Nathan and Jessica. I was far less privileged to know Nathan prior to meeting Jessica. Here in the South, we have developed a certain vernacular to describe the human condition that is particular to our way of life. Nathan, as we say, was once a heathen. Even worse, he was a rancorous, which we shorten to "ranc," heathen. It was bad. He's a lot to handle now, for heaven's sakes, I guess because of the residue from his heathen days.

And then, as we say in our region, Nathan "found Jesus." Or Jesus found Nathan. Something fired up in the region of his brain that we call the heart, and everything changed. He joined a church, got a steady job, became successful and generous, married Jessica, bought a house, had children. He's not a heathen anymore; he's just a boring middle-aged Christian adult with thinning hair and a mortgage. We are working on toning down the profanity in Atlanta traffic, but other than that the lion has been tamed. Nathan is a good *homo sapiens*.

While officiating Nathan and Jessica's wedding, I choked up for a moment. It wasn't the ceremony that got to me; it was witnessing the image of God in this man, in this couple. "For better or for worse," they recited. "Until death do us part." Crazy words. "Love is anarchy. Love is chaos," writes the literary critic Claire Dederer.[2] This tumor business allows him to prove the mettle of those anarchic words, and it is beautiful.

Nathan must feed his wife. He gives her water to drink. He puts her shoes on for her and walks her around the block a dozen times per day. He does not sleep. He encourages her in the hope that she can process his words. He hangs on every grunt and glance. He asks her if she is comfortable. He asks her if she wants a hug. "Love is patient," St. Paul wrote, and he wasn't even referring to a brain surgery patient. "God is love," St. John wrote, and that is what is going on here.

Yesterday, I craned my neck from the living room to watch Nathan and Jessica in the kitchen. He was feeding her. Then he stopped, grasped her hand, leaned forward in his chair to the point where I thought he was getting down on one knee, and he looked into the eyes of his bride. And his eyes were not filled with regret or pain or even sympathy, but with wonder. I had seen that precise look before, years ago, at the altar where they wed.

And tears sprung in my eyes as I thought to myself, "Oh my God. That's what this story is about."

I don't know why things happen as they do. I don't believe God causes everything, like some brute force. I do believe He is involved in ways that are often indecipherable to us. Jesus said that God cares for every sparrow and has numbered the hairs on our heads. Of course, sparrows are still preyed upon and hair falls out from chemotherapy, but even brain tumors cannot undo the strange plan that God has for us, the plan to reflect the image of his goodness to every dark corner of this world.

"Now these three remain: faith, hope and love," Paul wrote in words that have echoed over ten thousand weddings, "but the greatest of these is love." When it is all stripped bare, we are the glorious

2. Dederer, *Monsters: A Fan's Dilemma*, 257.

homo sapiens: big-brained creatures with the capacity, the daily opportunity, to reflect the image of God through the way that we love. I suppose God could have eviscerated Jessica's brain tumor just as we prayed that he would. But I think that would pale in comparison to the miracle that I am watching unfold now.

The middle is so different from the early years of marriage, those days of heat, tumult, adjustment. In the middle, you are already adjusted. The problems are different. In the middle, it's the tumors that have been latent for a long while, waiting undercover, that you have to deal with.

In Genesis, the story of Abram really covers some distance. So much transpires—the covenant of circumcision, the destruction of Sodom and Gomorrah, more pimping out Sarah—that it's easy to forget the crux of the story. Again, Abram's name means "Father." He is supposed to have children, to birth a great nation that will bless the world. As if to rub it in, God even renames him Abraham along the way, which means "Father of Many." I'm not saying that God toys with people for the heck of it, but his pace sure can seem cruel.

And then, with Abraham a hundred and Sarah ninety, the promise is born. Oh, joy begin. It is so ridiculous that they name the child Laughter. One Jewish legend calls it the greatest day in the history of the world:

> The whole world rejoiced, for God remembered all barren women at the same time with Sarah. They all bore children. And all the blind were made to see, all the lame were made whole, the dumb were made to speak, and the mad were restored to reason. And a still greater miracle happened: on the day of Isaac's birth the sun shone with such splendor as had not been seen since the fall of man, and as he will shine again only in the future world.[3]

You would think that in the face of such a miraculous gift, all would be giggles and gratitude for the happy couple. Abraham even throws a giant feast the day that Isaac was weaned. This is

3. Ginzberg, *Legends of the Jews*, 82.

their first and only together, so every milestone and moment are cause for celebration. But something has been gnawing at Sarah. There is a tumor growing from a conscious decision that they both made years ago. The tension for Sarah is not that Abraham had a former mistress, as this was her idea to begin with, but that the bastard child might get something from them.

The tension is (again) scarcity.

"That slave woman's son will never share in the inheritance with my son Isaac," Sarah announces, which the next sentence says "greatly distressed Abraham." There isn't enough to go around for both of them, Sarah says. We must withhold.

We have seen that this is not uncommon in the middle of life. What is new is that it is also not uncommon in the middle of marriage.

A few months ago, I celebrated twenty years of marriage. I have been together with my wife for more years of my life than I have not. Of course, it has not been easy and we know what the brink is like, but here we are, happy. I'm glad that stories like Abraham and Sarah are in the Bible because they remind me that reasonable happiness is sufficient, and if you want to move toward ebullient happiness, you're going to have to deal with some tumors.

Many of these daily tumors are predictable: apathy, boredom, selfishness, laziness. But there is one that is long-term and a killer. It has been growing inside your brain since the day you were born. It is the tumor of misorientation.

In 1878, Lieutenant George De Long led the crew of the USS Jeannette toward the Arctic Cap, destined, so they thought, to be the first to reach the famed North Pole. The ship was imbued with all of the latest technologies and the crew was experienced. The problem, they would discover, was their map. Using maps drawn by Dr. August Henrich Petermann, they looked for a "thermometric gateway" through the ice, but none existed. They had to instead "shed its organizing ideas, in all their unfounded romance, and to replace them with a reckoning of the way the Arctic truly is."[4] They had to shed their preordained map and deal with reality. Marriage is like this, especially in the middle.

One of the earliest examples of Chinese painting is called the Admonitions Scroll, on display in the British Museum today. In one depiction, the emperor turns away from his wife, rejecting her. There is a stenciled poem beside the scene:

> No one can please forever;
>
> When love has reached its highest pitch,
> it changes its object;
>
> For whatever has reached fullness must decline.
>
> This law is absolute.[5]

This is not the map of marriage that we want. It is simply the map. And so we read it, and we navigate.

I will say this: the map is full of tumors, and the tumors are fed by scarcity, by withholding. Like Sarah withheld from Ishmael, we hold so much back. We withhold our approval, our elation, our margins. We withhold emotion, praise, words. We withhold happiness from our very selves. We blame the bastard child, but we know he was our idea and it is all our fault.

And then, sometimes, we resect these tumors, and we get down on our knees, and we see, and it is pure wonder. Wendell Berry phrased it as only he can, "And once again I am blessed, choosing again what I chose before."[6]

4. Sides, *In the Kingdom of Ice*, 163.

5. MacGregor, *A History of the World in 100 Objects*, 255.

6. Berry, *The Selected Poems of Wendell Berry*, 198.

15

Testing: Losing Our Narratives

"Some time later, God tested Abraham."—Genesis 22:1

"This is the kingdom of God, the kingdom of danger
and of risk, of eternal beginning and eternal becoming,
of opened spirit and of deep realization, the kingdom of
holy insecurity."—Martin Buber

I RAN ON THE cross-country team in college because I was not
good enough to play any real sports and I thought that if I could
get a scholarship I wouldn't have to get a third job flipping burg-
ers or mopping floors. It was fun traveling and socializing and
eating out for free and the rest was more or less hell. And remember, I like running.

We had two practices per day for the duration of the season,
conditioning for months before the first meet. The practices were at
6:00 AM and 4:00 PM. I missed one morning practice in all those
years, and the coach was screaming on my answering machine. We
were barely a winning team, and this was serious business.

The hard part is that you never knew what sort of practice
torture you were going to get. One morning he might sprint you
on a track until you threw up the last night's dinner. In the evenings he sometimes took us to a place called "the molehill," which
might as well have been Mount Everest beneath asphalt. Once a
week he told us to get in the back of his pickup, and he just drove

out into the country, dropped us on the side of the road, and drove away. All this started in September, when the east Tennessee heat and humidity may as well have been the Florida Everglades. Again, I like running, and I have no nostalgia for these things.

The point, of course, was to condition us by testing us. We were always being tested, always being timed. "Rice, do you enjoy being last?" was a way of communicating that I was not doing well on the test. Eventually, the tests prepare you. The very word, *test*, originally meant to ascertain the quality of a metal by melting it in a cauldron. When you're tested, you learn what you're really made of.

And it's no surprise that contest includes the word test. If you are going to run against the big cats, you better know your mettle, and you better come ready.

On Easter Sunday last year, in the middle of the Covid-19 pandemic, my family and I got up early, attended our sunrise service on the computer, then the Easter service on the TV. Around lunchtime, it started to rain, then kept it up most of the day. It was then that I realized the dire nature of the situation. The night before, I had finished all the books that I had been reading. I was out of books and the Barnes and Noble was not open on Easter.

In my house, we have a policy that we will go without food before we go without new books. We do not go to the library. I even have a personal policy: you can borrow my car, you can have the shirt off my back, you can live in my basement, but you cannot borrow any of my books. I do not loan them out. If Jesus needed a book on my shelf, he would have to buy his own, it's just the policy. So I bit the bullet and rode my bike up to Target, which I figured was open, to find a book from their very poor and pedestrian selection on Easter, Easter of all days! It was like trading a steak dinner for Taco Bell. Target was closed. My countenance dropped further, for I had only one much worse option left. If I was going to buy a book to read on Easter I would have to buy it from the Kroger, the Kroger! The Kroger just has a little stand by the magazines with a few dumb inspirational books that aren't even inspirational; they're just dumb. So I gave up, went home, and picked up a book that my wife had been reading. I feared it was for women only but I was wrong. It was a good book which meant that Easter was not ruined.

The book is by a Christian author in Canada named Sarah Bessey who was in a terrible car crash that left her in constant chronic pain. Before the accident, she went to her mailbox one day and found an invitation from the Vatican to go to Rome to participate in an inter-denominational assembly of Christian leaders to meet and worship with Pope Francis. She was an evangelical, very suspicious of Catholic Christianity, but thought that she should take this remarkable opportunity. So two months after this accident, even though she could only walk for short amounts of time and, even then, in considerable pain, she and her husband flew to Rome.

They were waiting in the Vatican for the worship service with the Pope when they suddenly met two Catholic priests who also were from Canada. The priests had come to the Vatican that week for no other reason than they felt like the Lord spoke to them and told them to go on these days. They start talking and one of these priests says to her, and I quote, "Sarah, Father Harold and I sense God wants you to experience healing. Is there something going on in your body?" And they began to touch and to speak to, her spine, specific vertebrae, left hip, neck, saying to each body part, "Move, Lord."[1] And she testified that every bit of pain stopped right that second. She flew back home with zero pain.

For those of us who grew up thinking that Catholics were no more saved than Mormons, this is a lot to stomach. I was even more rattled by the punch line: for several months she was completely healed, without pain, and then it all came back, constant and searing pain, just as it was before. Here is what she wrote about the unraveling of her healing, her unhealing: "I had wanted to have more control of my narrative of God."[2]

1. Bessey, *Miracles and Other Reasonable Things*, 112–113.
2. Bessey, *Miracles and Other Reasonable Things*, 156.

The word that comes to mind is singular in scope: the story is full of *pathos*. No other word will do. The text itself weeps. "No story in Genesis is as terrible, as powerful, as mysterious, as elusive as this one," Leon Kass writes.[3] It is too much to take, this God who makes outlandish promises come to pass, who is better than our best dreams, who crushes us to pieces. "Oh stormy, violent, burning surging love," the mystic Bernard of Clairvaux wrote. "You tear down orders, pay no heed to ancestry, know no measures. Propriety, reason, modesty, counsel, judgment—all these you make your prisoners."[4] We know that this is true, and we hate what such love takes from us, and we hate what it makes us give.

God calls Abraham, makes him wait, destroys cities, makes a covenant, makes him wait, fulfills his every desire, and now will slaughter the old man's heart like a sacrifice to Molech.

In Jewish tradition, the story is known simply as the *akeda*, the binding, the only place the Hebrew word is found in the entire Bible. "To find the true meaning of Aggadah," wrote Abraham Joshua Heschel, "search deeply into each interpretation. You will find there struggles, worries, and yearnings, eternal problems and contemporary questions, the travails of community and individual that vexed both the Sages and the nation as a whole."[5]

"Take your son, your only son, Isaac, whom you love, and go to the region of Moriah. Sacrifice him there as a burnt offering on one of the mountains I will tell you about."

"Your only son," God twists the knife. In the Talmud, God demarcates "whom you love" in answer to Abraham's initial response: "Which one?" The tradition weeps:

> Said God to him: "Take, I beg you—please—Your son."
> "Which son? I have two sons" he said. "Your only son,"
> replied He. "This one is the only one of his mother, and
> this one is the only one of his mother." "The one you
> love"—"Is there a limit to the affections?" "Isaac" said He.

3. Kass, *The Beginning of Wisdom: Reading Genesis*, 333.

4. Solle, *The Silent Cry*, 117.

5. Heschel, *Heavenly Torah as Refracted Through the Generations*, 7.

The rabbis made the story more painful, not less.

Elie Wiesel tells the story of a group of Jews on a train to die in Auschwitz and a rabbi hunched in the middle of the packed boxcar. He began to speak to the group about a particular tradition that when the Messiah came, He would organize a dance for the righteous. He then explained that *dance* and *forgive* are words that share a root. He said that one day there would come a time when they, if they survived, would dance and forgive God for it all. I ask you, if we never had the Jews, who would tell us the truth about this life, about our pain?

I think of others, contending with God for a fledgling nation in the throes of loss. Nelson Mandela sits imprisoned on Robbin Island all those years, fighting to shelter the faint glimmer of hope. Abraham Lincoln spends untold blood to hold the Union together by a thread, all the while suffering the death of his own son. God the Father on Good Friday, as we all of us publicly lynched the son of love. That same son had famously prayed, "And lead us not into the test."

But test God can, and test God will.

It was once popular to interpret this story as the Bible's rather dramatic mechanism for disassociating the God of Israel with the ancient practice of child sacrifice. This would be comforting and safe. But only a few Jewish interpreters ever did that and perhaps none before Joseph Ibn Kaspi in the fourteenth century CE. The Talmud says that Isaac was a full-fledged adult of thirty-three years old when Abraham bound him on Mount Moriah (remind you of someone?). In reality, testing is such a consistent theme throughout the Bible that it leads us to places where we do not wish to go, to the grave demands of God.

We don't know what to do with this anymore, because we have so sanitized and domesticated divinity. We have created religion apart from this irascible God. We have theologized our way out of Him, replacing wildness with safety. Civil religion does not test anything about you. You say the pledge, pay your taxes, and keep clean. Tolerance does not test anything about you. Secularism only requires that you do not flinch in the face of its totalitarian nothingness. These are our faiths.

But God isn't easy. God tests. This God demands. This God requires. As Walter Brueggemann writes, "Testing is unnecessary in religions of tolerance. The testing times for Israel and for all of us who are heirs of Abraham are those times when it is seductively attractive to find an easier, less demanding alternative to God."[6]

I remember the day I found myself on Mount Moriah at the end of every dream. It was a Tuesday afternoon. I was sitting at my desk at the church where I was the senior pastor. It was just a few months prior to getting lost in the woods. My breath was short, my pulse elevated, sweat running down my back. I felt something like a mixture of total exhaustion and pure panic.

I thought I was having a heart attack, all 160 pounds of me.

And believe it or not, not much is wrong. The church was struggling along but alright, our kids were babies, we were both in school. But besides the typical pressures from this stage of life, everything is pretty much normal. The story would be better if I had previously joined a street gang or day-traded away our life savings. But any such elements of high drama are nonexistent; barely any of low drama for that matter. I was surrounded by people who loved me, including my wife, had a good job and a house on a golf course, and my emotional stability ground to a screeching halt.

In fact, it was Father Abraham holding a dagger above my exposed chest. I know it was a test because of what it made me learn.

I am convinced that we live our lives according to formulas that are almost always implicit and unstated. They can be very difficult to discern even though they drive almost everything about us. Someone bouncing from relationship to relationship has a formula. Addicts have formulas. Someone who wins the gold medal in an Olympic event got there through a formula. Formulas can be good or bad, and most are in between.

My formula was simple: apply pressure to myself = achieve desired result. I began constructing this formula in the second

6. Brueggemann, *Genesis*, 190.

grade when I went from being a dumb kid who the doctors thought could have a learning disability to earning straight A's for the prize of a blue honor roll ribbon (recognition, really). I know that seems overly simple, but that's where it started. Over time, I could depend on the formula like breathing. I made straight A's, straight every-thing forever. Make the grade, climb the ladder, win the thingy. Self-induced pressure was my performance-enhancing drug. It always worked. Whatever I wanted or needed, I could just ratchet up the pressure and I would get it. I was always in control.

And then God roots around in our formulas like the trash dumpsters they are, agitating the contents, breaking things apart. In the Bible, this is hero-making. Young, strong Moses stands with his hands held high over the Egyptian he has killed. He is ready to lead the revolution for his people against slavery. God takes him to the desert, spends forty years breaking those formu-las of youth and strength like a wild stallion. When he is decrepit, literally stammering and scared, he is ready. David is anointed by the prophet Samuel as king over Israel, the underdog story for the ages, the militia captain who will one day lead the nation in righteousness and justice, the harbinger of the very Son of God. Buzzed high off of his aptitude for risk and reward, carrying the head of Goliath as a trophy, God takes him to the desert, where he will flee and scrap for his life for years. When he has learned to trust, he is ready. Even Jesus emerges from His baptism, validated by the very voice of God: "This is my beloved Son, whom I love. With him I am well pleased." Surely now He will take over the world! Instead, God takes him to the desert, where he will learn something of how deep the fight will be.

Break the formula, change the narrative.

I searched a dozen English Bibles and not one translation has the word *formula* in it. The Bible uses a different word: *idol*. Idols are instruments of control, and they are both just high-definition illusions, smoke, mirrors, and bunk. Idols fleece our formulas with the sanctimony of God, but God isn't there, just the sanctimony.

And I know that this is difficult to comprehend, but maybe the point of this disturbing ancient story of near filicide is that not even our *moral* formulas can take the place of God. He demands to supersede everything that is impersonal, however ethical it might be. Soren Kierkegaard describes the dilemma: "At every moment, Abraham can stop; he can repent of the whole thing as a spiritual trial; then he can speak out, and everyone will be able to understand him—but then he is no longer Abraham."[7]

The only formulas God seems to care about are the ones that he shatters like all his heroes.

Anne Lamott lists "the three most terrible truths of our existence: that we are so ruined, and so loved, and in charge of so little."[8] There are no formulas, just a wild narrative with the God who defies them.

---

7. Kierkegaard, *Fear and Trembling*, 115.
8. Lamott, *Help, Thanks, Wow*, 27.

16

Providence: Rams Along the Winding Way

Abraham looked up and there in a thicket he saw a ram caught by its horns. He went over and took the ram and sacrificed it as a burnt offering instead of his son. So Abraham called that place The Lord Will Provide. And to this day it is said, "On the mountain of the Lord it will be provided."—Genesis 22:13–14

"There are deep problems with affirming that God both tests and provides. The problems are especially acute for those who seek a 'reasonableness' in their God. But this text does not flinch before nor pause at the unreasonableness of this story. God is not a logical premise who must perform in rational consistency."—Walter Brueggemann

FOR MANY, MAKING A sports team is a rite of passage growing up, a major point of pride. High school kids endure punishing conditioning trying to make the next round of cuts, like an episode of *Survivor*. There is always a league that will fit any skill level, but that's not the point. Neither is the sport. The point, really, is making the team, proving yourself to people. The point is our need for something far beyond individual achievement.

Cross-country running as an organized sport, however, which typically begins in high school, is different than the others. This is a sport that is often conducted in service to other sports, the "real" ones that fans want to see. Believe it or not, athletes in other sports are often *sentenced* to run cross country to improve their conditioning or just because they mouthed off. I saw a T-shirt at a race: "My Sport is Your Sport's Punishment." Yep.

I had such a teammate in college, a freshman basketball player who was on the brink of getting kicked off the team for excessive partying or bad grades, or both. I hate to be stereotypical, but he may be the only true jock that I have ever really met, an unbelievably jocular jock. He was not much for conversation, seemed dumbfounded and lost (hungover?) in the middle of the day, always with a touristy look on his face, yet was a fierce competitor. His whole demeanor changed at the races. I can't imagine he had ever run distances before, and he could put his head down and run you into the ground.

We were at a regional meet on the campus of our conference leader when he exploded off the line. I stayed in his draft, keeping up, then fell back a bit. It's usually not wise to be in first place during the initial mile, but there he was by himself, pulling away by fifty yards. I noticed the better teams nodding and smirking. Suddenly the course dropped and narrowed to the left, a hair pin turn that had us guarding our kidneys (it wasn't ice hockey, but miscreants were known to take the occasional shot. In this sport, there are no referees.). We careened to the left, and the jock just kept going straight. He never looked back, just shot straight into the woods like a bullet. I saw him again when we got in the van to go home.

Like I said before, I have seen that slogan on bumper stickers, "Not all who wander are lost." Well, that may be true, but a bunch of them sure do seem to be.

Abraham raises the knife.

When I had my children, my brain turned to pudding, my heart to mush, never to return. I was taken, smitten, and still am, just over the moon. They have lately just turned into teenagers, and I don't care what everyone says, I think it is absolutely rapturous. Every stage of their lives has been a dream. They are the only thing in my life that makes me cry. I am crying now, just writing these words.

Abraham raises the knife.

This is the lunacy of this story, the longing of Abraham's heart. If I heard voices in my head telling me to do this, I certainly hope that someone would have the good sense to shoot me or at least to straightjacket me and put me, mumbling and drooling, in a locked-door institution. In the book of Judges, Jephthah is mocked for the stupidity of child sacrifice. For heaven's sakes, God himself sometimes mocks the ever-popular Canaanite Baal cult for the practice, asserting that this is "something I did not commend or mention, nor did it enter my mind" (Jeremiah 19:5; 32:35).

Abraham raises the knife. Who would not hesitate, yet the point of the story is that he will do the deed. He will do whatever it takes. It is madness. He will revert to the status of humanity before the fall. He will not probe as Adam and Eve who, along with the serpent, embraced their individuality. He will not ask about his choices. He will not extrapolate a moral framework upon God as he once had. The one who was hailed by centuries of rabbis for his courage to bargain with God to save a condemned city of vicious rapists is too tired now, or too faithless, or too broken to save his own son. "The absence of lament makes a religion of coercive obedience the only possibility," Brueggemann writes, and this is all that is left.[1] Abraham barely even speaks in the narrative, just the same one-word response twice—*hinneni*—"Behold, me." He does not even utter a verb. Jean Renoir once wrote into his film that the "one awful thing" in this world "is that everyone has his reasons,"[2] but Abraham has none now. The young vision of the stars has been exhausted and he should have never believed any of it anyway. So he will surrender his humanity and the whole world just to blindly obey. He will set the flame and burn it all, remorseless. He has surrendered not just his will, but his mind, comatose. He will raise

---

1. Brueggemann, "The Costly Loss of Lament," 111.
2. Renoir, *La règle du jeu*, DVD.

the knife and plunge it deep. He will sacrifice the child of promise to pass a test that he cannot even discern.

Frederick Buechner writes, "If a *schlemiel* is a person who goes through life spilling soup on people and a *schlemozzle* is the one it keeps getting spilled on, then Abraham was a *schlemozzle*."[3] Perhaps Abraham intends this to be the end of the ordeal of his disastrous life. In English, this is so poignant: *disaster* at its Greek root means "the unraveling of stars." Abraham will vaporize the promise of the nation, the starry night. Will he turn the knife on himself?

And then, like a shooting star, the divine intervention. It had all been a test, utterly meaningless, unless God is a megalomaniac beyond human comprehension. And as a ram rustles in a thorn thicket, the second razor of the double-edged story befalls us, though the first one had already drawn blood.

God had all this planned in advance. It was rigged, thrown like the Black Sox series, paid off by the bookies. The death of Isaac was never meant to be. This was the death of something else. "In its stark horror and ambiguous statements," Tikva Frymer-Kenskey writes, "the story of the *Akeda* remains the central text in the formation of our spiritual consciousness."[4]

I read the Bible as a Christian, so I can't help that Jesus is something of a beautiful nag, beckoning and clouding my judgement. I recognize these Hebrew texts as Hebrew, and I try to read them on their own terms. They are Jewish texts first, and a gift to anyone else. That only seems respectful, like appropriately deferring to local customs when you visit a different country. Yet Jesus is a haunt, always there, a lens, a prism. I can hardly read any part of Abraham's story, any ancient text for that matter, without the connections to Christ growing like weeds and like flowers.

In one of the most primitive and earliest stories about Jesus in the first Gospel written, he is with his disciples on a boat in the Sea of Galilee. "And there arose a great storm of wind," the King James reads, so that water flooded into the boat, nearly swamping the hull.

3. Buechner, *Beyond Words*, 3.
4. Frymer-Kenskey, "Akeda: A View From the Bible," 144.

And where is Jesus? In the very flooding hull, sound asleep. As if this were not enough, Mark's Gospel includes one of the most wondrous details in the Bible: "with his head on a cushion." In the annals of history, we are the recipients of no description of that lovely and condemned head, but here it is exhausted, drenched, sinking into the sea at perfect peace, on a cushion.

Famously, we know what happens next. The rather irritated Lord of glory rebukes the storm and it ceases, like an angry child set to bed. My point is not all that, but the reaction of the disciples, who the text says were "terrified."

They said, "Who is this?"

St. Augustine said in a sermon, "Even when he reveals himself, God remains a mystery beyond words. If you understood Him, it would not be God."

I didn't grow up in the theological tradition of Calvinism. Calvinism doesn't jibe well with being American, and perhaps we have never even seen a true Calvinist in the South. Calvinism focuses on the sovereignty of God, that God is in control of things, and we Southerners are fine with that in the big, historic picture. But we also believe that God created us to control our own destinies, that God helps those who help themselves, and so on. We have found a way to love Jesus and to also consider the idea that someone else is writing our story to be odious. Most of us are Republicans down here, so it all fits together.

When I endured the demise of what I held so dear, the deconstruction of my treasure that had been so sure, I didn't blame God for one second. I prayed, took comfort in the Scriptures, and trusted that things were up to me. Unlike Abraham, I didn't worry about the meaning of it all. I just put one foot in front of the other, like a running trail. I chose the paths, could turn where I wished, figured stuff out. I was sure that nothing that happened to me could unravel the historical reality of Easter, and that God was fine and loved me, but it was a rather sentimental, sanitized sort of love. When God is safe, like a Hallmark card, life is pretty straightforward and more or less up to you.

The ram in the thicket sure complicates this precious equation, bless my little Southern heart. John Calvin himself once wrote, "Without knowledge of God there is no knowledge of self." Oh, this hard providence.

It was not until years later, and heartbreak and pain and professional counseling, that it all hit me. All of these scenes I had been living, these bits and pieces, fits and starts, all of these narrative threads added up to something that I did not at all intend, something far bigger than me. In Anne Rice's novel about the boyhood of Jesus, he prays to God: "Father in Heaven, tell me what you want of me. Tell me what all these things mean? *Everything has a story to it*. And what is the story of all this?"[5] Those moments where it seemed like I had just accidentally shot off into the woods off course were a part of the story. There was purpose, reason, thick meaning in the fury. Not one step had, in fact, been wandering. In a moment, like the end of an M. Night Shyamalan movie when nothing has made any sense until it all does, my blindness gave way to piercing sight.

I had been a bit player in a drama so minute, so detailed, that it was I myself that was discovering it, from the inside of the script. I had been unwittingly enrolled in Pain College then Forgiveness University, course by course, for this is life, and only at graduation did I grasp the curriculum and its designer. That was the day I stood in the boat with the disciples, gasping for breath. "Who is this?"

That is the sort of moment that Abraham must have had when he saw that God had provided the ram. *Provide* is such a beautiful word, from the Latin *pro-video*, "to see before." One ancient Jewish midrash says that Abraham's ram was created at dusk on the sixth day of creation, the last moment before the creation of the Sabbath, and then just waited all those centuries for God to reveal, to provide it at Moriah. We have tended to think about providing as giving a gift, and providence as God's jurisdiction over our lives. But provision and providence are really the same word, the same thing. Paul Tillich articulates the link:

5. Rice, *Christ the Lord*, 252.

Faith in divine Providence is that faith that nothing can prevent us from fulfilling the ultimate meaning of our existence. Providence does not mean a divine planning by which everything is predetermined, as is an efficient machine. Rather, Providence means that there is a creative and saving possibility implied in every situation, which cannot be destroyed by any event. Providence means that the daemonic and destructive forces within ourselves and our world can never have an unbreakable grasp upon us, and that the bond which connects us with the fulfilling love can never be disrupted.[6]

The ram died instead of Isaac, but that's not really the point at all. What really died was some little piece of Abraham that still stumbled to trust this wild God. What was really being tested was not Abraham's obedience, but his willingness to trust, or at least to wrestle. That was the point of the ram's sacrifice; it was a feast, a celebration, a baptism. During the meal, God once again swears by himself that he will bless the whole world through Abraham because he had passed the trust test.

It is the last time in the entire narrative that God speaks to Abraham.

"Who is this?"

---

6. Tillich, *The Shaking of the Foundations*, 106–107.

17

Intimacy: Running Away

The Hittites replies to Abraham, "Sir, listen to us. You are a mighty prince among us. Bury your dead in the choicest of our tombs. None of us will refuse you his tomb for burying your dead."—Genesis 23:6

"We have lost a sense of wonder at the physical world we inhabit. Our food has lost its taste, our labor has lost its joy, and our most intimate physical experiences have lost their beauty, their romance, their intimacy, their holiness."—Rabbi Lavey Derby

SPORTS ARE MENTAL, LIKE everything else in life. In fact, each individual sport has developed specific terminology to describe the optimal mental state, that plane of perceiving and moving that elevates an athlete to a point of dominance. Rowing teams call it achieving a state of "flow." Basketball players are "in the zone." Baseball hitters are "dialed in." In such a state of mind, athletes will often describe a change in their perception of the time-space continuum. The crowd is screaming, but for them all is quiet. The world around them slows down. They do not perceive existence outside of their field of focus, like a camera lens. For many, it is not winning that drives them, but chasing this feeling, this competitive nirvana.

Distance running has this status too, but it is more pronounced. After all, unlike most other sports, running is the whole body just doing one thing, over and over. The interconnections have to be perfect to achieve the runner's high. It is dependent on a host of factors: what you have been eating, your hydration, the quality of your sleep, the levels of your stress, whether you have forgiven someone. This is why running can be so spiritual: it is all of you at once, warts, baggage, brawn, with no timeouts. And all of this is being processed in your brain, which rarely finds peace with so many signals to interpret. As a famous saying in the long-distance community goes, "Ultrarunning is 90 percent mental. The other 10 percent, that's mental too."

But there are those moments when the peace settles in, chemical bliss drifting down from your brain into your extremities. And it is quiet, the world is radiant, and you slip into a Zen state like a good dream. It can happen anytime anywhere, but for me, it is usually at 4:00 in the morning during the summer, when time is at its most placid, or on a single-track trail in the woods, perhaps in a line of racers or alone, on autopilot.

It is good for running, but bad for life in the middle. It is solitary confinement. It requires being locked inside your head.

Somewhere along the way, I started to struggle, deeply, at the level of the soul. The signs have always been there. I was a teenager in the nineties when it was cool to brood, and, though I was gregarious, people would comment on why I looked so sad. It was in college when my roommate first used the dreaded term: "People think you are locked inside your head all the time." Add that to a competitive intensity that is insatiable, and we have ourselves here a recipe for problems.

But I fell in love. Heck, I plunged in it, like an anvil thrown into the ocean. I dated a lot in high school and college and never thought much of any of it. Then I saw the girl who would become my wife in the back of a room in a church, and Atlantis rose out of the sea, and after one date, in my mind, it was just a done deal. Thunderstruck. It was love at first sight, the textbooks be damned.

Now that we are in the middle, our marriage has been pretty normal, so far as I can tell. There have been highs and lows, conditionality and unconditionality. We have struggled plenty and yet we have shared some ecstasy too. We have really good kids, an affordable house, some money to do things we want to do. We are mostly stable, yet I am still locked inside my head too often. It ebbs and flows.

You have probably heard of "locked-in syndrome." It is a worst nightmare, like an Edgar Allen Poe plot. Back then, people feared being buried alive, so much so that they put instruments in the graves that would allow those who might have been errantly declared deceased to call above ground for help. Modern medicine has created a far worse reality: given just the right accident or aneurysm and you could be buried within yourself, never to return.

Think about it, if you can: total uninterrupted consciousness, but without the ability to move, speak, or respond. Wouldn't anyone rather just be hurled into the sea?

It is a metaphor, of course, but I know something of what this is like.

In Genesis 23, with ram's meat still on Abraham's breath, Sarah dies. We have few details, only that she was 127, and Abraham is lying beside the corpse, and that is a winsome detail, isn't it? He is lying there and mourning over her, the text says. "These hundred years, my beloved." He does not know what to do.

This loneliness has been building for some time. Isaac did not accompany his father, understandably, down the mountain called Moriah. In fact, Abraham never utters another word to Isaac in the narrative after chapter 22. The patriarch goes to live in Beersheba alone. Some ancient interpreters wrote that Sarah died when she heard Abraham had taken their son up the mountain to be sacrificed. What happened on that mountain separated everyone. And something in the aftermath locked the old man inside of himself.

The rest of the chapter is banal and pointless. It *should* be a poem, a symphony, an ode to lifelong love. It should take your breath away, grieving the one who laughed to start the epic journey they have had. Instead, the mourning stops, and Sarah is an afterthought.

You would think the story would be about the death of the poor man's wife, but it's not. It's about the poor man's pride.

I have noticed in the middle that emotions are not typically what they once were. The highs and lows are more muted. At worse, it is just easier to go about the daily business and try not to feel much. I think this is why men start drinking themselves to death, or buy Corvettes, or take on a mistress, trying to feel, searching out any key that might unlock them from inside of their own heads.

Abraham can only feel so much before he gets back to daily business, and the remainder of what we know about Sarah's time above ground is just a bunch of silly haggling over who is to pay for the cave. It's so dumb it hardly bears repeating, this rather unsophisticated historical one-upmanship. The Hittites want to give Abraham a burial cave for free. He demands to pay the cave's value so as not to cede the social high ground. The requisite ancient near-eastern back-and-forth ensues. Abraham wins whatever there is to win, pays for the cave, and buries Sarah. It never even says that he mourned again. He just got the cave and moved on.

That's what it feels like to be locked inside your head. You just move on.

I lost a friend who I love, and I am fearful of a day that I might receive a dreadful phone call. We became friends in college over politics and music, started a band called The Fabulous, and played around a bit. Even as I moved around the country we stayed friends for twenty years. He called to check up on me. He traveled to take me golfing on my birthday. He helped me move more than once. We talked on the phone every week, but never talked about deep things like our feelings or our marriages. I know this seems tangential, but there was just a loyalty, a feeling to the friendship that reminded me of that scene in *Tombstone* where Doc Holiday is suffering from tuberculosis, yet riding with Wyatt Earp to watch his back, simply because they are friends. "Hell, I got lots of friends," someone says to Doc. I love his response, and I identify with it too: "I don't."

But my friend was an only child and had a pretty severe disease that often laid him low, and he was also painfully introverted. One day, he just drifted inside his head one last time, and, so far as I know, he has never come out. We played golf the month before and everything was normal. Then he just moved out of his house on a Tuesday, stopped responding to anybody. This was not a midlife crisis. He kept his day job, didn't date or party, was not a drinker. He just moved on.

I would have to think more about anything else that I am actually afraid of, but I think it's just my kids getting hurt and this. Death ranks a lower fear factor.

I have had to come to terms with this tendency to fade away, and I am still coming to terms with it. I don't have the kind that makes you just disembark from your responsibilities physically, mine is different. I can just live disembarked; courteous, faithful, helpful, and away. It must be like living, sometimes, with a perfectly pleasant vegetable.

What am I so afraid of? The usual suspects. Vulnerability, intimacy, being truly and fully known. Typing about my daughters makes me want to cry. Typing out the usual suspects makes my stomach churn. I would rather just go on being very nice.

This is the reality of life in the middle, that these choices constrict. When you are young and the world is your oyster, you are drawn to outward things, and you can hide what you need to, even for years of marriage. You are driven by prizes then, and you'll do anything to get them. Twenty years in, that's just not possible anymore, and you can't just keep moving on. Eventually, you have to deal with your stuff. You have lepers in your head and invalids in your heart, and you have to decide what to do with them. They are not going to let you alone.

"When a culture is no longer centered in a living and continually renewed relational process, it freezes into the It-world which is broken only intermittently by the eruptive, glowing deeds of solitary spirits," wrote the Jewish philosopher Martin Buber.[1] If you are locked inside your head, there are only third

1. Buber, *I and Thou*, 103.

person pronouns about people who are far removed. It is a safe place that will soon kill you.

What is the antidote to this? The bad news is that there is no cure for locked-in syndrome. The people who have it will never be reconnected. They will simply continue to exist, like conscious ghosts, barring a miracle. But most of us never reach that state like my friend did. For us, the tendencies can be managed.

When Pope John Paul II first appeared to the world on the balcony of St. Peter's, he just said, "Christ, Christ is the answer." Yes, it seems trite, but I know of no greater option. For all that we can't know about him, we certainly can know that he was vulnerability embodied, a man of vast intimacy, without hurry, whose relationships were characterized by joy. He was invited to dinner parties everywhere. He preferred touch to distance. He looked people in the eye. He observed flowers and birds and farms. He was curious about things big and small. He had long conversations with people who didn't matter in the eyes of society. He discerned how people were thinking. He played with children. He even found people like Zacchaeus up in the trees, because he had the interest to look in trees. He was pure and unadulterated joy.

He never just moved on.

The night before his lynching, Jesus shared a final meal with his most intimate friends, and I place an unnecessary comma here, to pause and think about what love must have filled the room. Three years after they first formed this band of brothers, they could finally eat together without a fistfight breaking out. They had traveled together, worked together, prayed together, laughed together and shared countless donated meals through the hospitality of strangers. Only this one was different, with the candlelight flickering across their faces. On this night, Jesus would institute a new meal, his meal, the hallmark of what would later become Christian worship.

It is sad what that meal has become. Veritable wars have been fought over the nature of this meal. Some traditions have worshipped the meal as if it were God himself. Others have reduced it to a little individual prayer moment tacked on to the middle of a numbingly repetitive guitar song. But at its core, the meal was not some magic means of forgiveness or just a way to remember Christ's death. The meal was about intimacy.

Henri Nouwen once again draws blood:

> When we eat together we are vulnerable to one another. Around the table we can't wear weapons of any sort. Eating from the same bread and drinking from the same cup call us to live in unity and peace. This becomes very visible when there is a conflict. Then eating and drinking together can become a truly threatening event . . . Don't you think that our desire to eat together is an expression of our even deeper desire to be food for one another?[2]

The next morning in the middle of his life, Jesus would be naked, suspended between heaven and earth, his heart ever open, supple, tender, attending to the needs of his mother and a bandit, seeking connection.

2. Nouwen, *Life of the Beloved*, 111.

18

Parenting: Learning to Let Go

Abraham was now very old, and the Lord had blessed him in every way. He said to the senior servant in his household, the one in charge of all that he had, "Put your hand under my thigh. I want you to swear by the Lord, the God of heaven and the God of earth, that you will not get a wife for my son from the daughters of the Canaanites, among whom I am living, but will go to my country and my own relatives and get a wife for my son Isaac."—Genesis 24:1–4

"We teach our children one thing only, as we were taught: to wake up. We teach our children to look alive there, to join by words and activities the life of human culture on the planet's crust. As adults we are almost all adept at waking up. We have so mastered the transition we have forgotten we ever learned it. Yet it is a transition we make a hundred times a day, as, like so many will-less dolphins, we plunge and surface, lapse and emerge. We live half our waking lives and all of our sleeping lives in some private, useless, and insensible waters we never mention or recall. Useless, I say. Valueless, I might add—until someone hauls their wealth up to the surface and into the wide-awake city, in a form that people can use."—Annie Dillard, *Teaching a Stone to Talk*

RUNNING ON TRAILS IN the woods is its own distinct art form. Most people probably don't even know it is a little cottage industry. These are not your Thanksgiving morning "gobble jogs" with thousands of soccer moms decked out in expensive jogging suits, encouraging one another. These are not the big city races where the police close the roads. Trail running spits out the amateurs quickly. Trail running is a culture unto itself, and you either know it or you don't.

I have come to love the people, the trail running community. They tend to be rugged. Lots of beards. They do not wear matching clothes or dress very intentionally, as they are there to get dirty. There is not near as much encouragement and a whole lot more introverts. At least until the whiskey bottle is passed around at the finish line, which is a trail scene thing.

For my first trail race, I showed up in road shoes. I did not know there were running shoes made for trails, and this was quickly pointed out to me. The trail shoes have metal plates in the right places, because the trails are dangerous. The running is technical. The miles are slower. People can really get hurt. Most of it is single track, meaning the trail is only wide enough for one person. You have to pay attention to the small colored markers that they put on the trees or you can find yourself lost. There are a hundred ways to have your day ruined, or much worse.

There is nothing like it.

Kristin Armstrong is an Olympic triathlete, a gold medalist three times over, even in her forties. Although most renowned for her dominant cycling, she reserves the spiritual language for running. "There is something magical about running," she said in an interview with *Runners World*. "After a certain distance, it transcends the body. Then a bit further, it transcends the mind. A bit further yet, and what you have before you, laid bare, is the soul."[1]

There is a certain flow, yes, to running down the center streets of a city in a herd of thousands. But road running is more of a physical test. It is about brute speed and going all out. The transcendence is on the trails. The Tarahumara Indians in Mexico have a

1. Barber, *Full Circle*, 121.

saying: "When you run on the earth and with the earth, you can run forever."[2] On the trails, the earth and our earthiness can be felt. The greenery, the changes in temperature and humidity, the quality and purity of the oxygen, the swells and dips. There is nothing like dropping down into a canyon, gravity causing legs to be effortless, feet landing softly on the dirt, the earth primitive and alive all around. This is why the ultramarathons are almost all on trails.

But there also climbs. What goes down must come up. And they can be dreadful. So dreadful that they are typically advertised in advance, so one can gird up thy loins.

This is the push and the pull of trail running, the give and the take. The climbs can be miles long and hundreds of feet. The erratic slopes and uneven ground take a toll on the body and the will. Looking straight up the mountain, it can seem like the climb will never end.

The climb is the price of the transcendence down the other side. And this is like parenting in the middle.

"Abraham was now very old, and the Lord had blessed him in every way" (24:1). These are the good years, the fat years. This is retirement in West Palm Beach, and golf and naps. Firmly planted in Canaan, Abraham is done moving around all of the time. Not just old but "very old," Abraham is almost finished with running.

The problem is that someone else is getting older too: Isaac, the very child of promise. Abraham knows that he is losing control, so he reasserts it.

We have already explored the unfortunate connection between comfort and control. Control is related to scarcity. They are the same, rooted in fear.

He calls in not just any servant, but the general manager. Talk about serious, he makes the GM hold the old man's testicles ("put your hand under my thigh" is a Hebrew euphemism) and pronounce the name of God not once but twice. The servant must be anticipating a monumental assignment, a major wealth transfer or some other weighty matter of Abraham's estate. Instead,

2. McDougall, *Born to Run*, 114.

Abraham wants to arrange the right kind of marriage for Isaac, and he wants to do it right now.

For the record, Abraham has given no thought in any of these texts to his own people from way back when. For the entire Genesis narrative, these people have represented all that he left behind to gain the promise to begin with. It seems odd to return the promise himself back to that place. But this is Abraham's will, and the chief servant will comply. "So the servant left, taking with him ten of his master's camels loaded with all kinds of good things" (v. 10), and he found Rebekah, and according to the last verse of the chapter, they were sorely happy.

Compared to our time, Abraham just got lucky, because adolescence as a social category didn't exist in the ancient near east. Try forcing such a thing on a modern western teenager and you will find yourself in a fix. Or try forcing anything at all. But some things that seem new aren't at all. Even in a culture where arranged adolescent marriages may have been the norm, the Talmud speaks of the *tzaar gidul banim*—the "pain of raising children."

Having children is rapturous, like falling in love with an ache. "There are three partners in the creation of all people: The Holy One, their father and their mother," say the sages in the Talmud. Never have I felt the goodness of God so strongly as when looking into the eyes of my daughters. When they were little, I wrote them a letter:

> Sophia, I will never forget holding you for the first time, my firstborn child, looking into the eyes of this little angelic baby for the first time, you the size of a football, a little angel football, crowned, as Jesus said, "a little lower than the angels." In that moment a question settled into my mind until the tears flowed, that beautiful firstborn question: "How could God be this good to me?"
>
> Evie, and then there was the second-born moment. This moment was a couple of years in the making in a sense; a couple of years of figuring out what it actually means to steward a miracle, a miracle who kept us awake at all hours of the night and vomited all over us at all hours of the most inopportune times. And then you appeared

in our midst, a second angelic visitation. And we found that the second-born question is even grander than the first. No longer, "How could God be this good *to me?*" But even more, "How could God be *this good?*" Period.

This extravagance is more than I can bear. There are days with you in which I fear I will wake up and it will all have been a dream; a breathlessly happy dream. The joy that you have brought to your mother and me is, in the words of 1 Peter 1:8, "unspeakable, and full of glory."

What I mean to say is that when I am with you, it as if the New Testament vision of creation has been finally consummated. I live my days now in a bright fog of wonder, feeling my way through a world made new each day, a world pulsing with the laughter of God. The theologians tell us that we live in what they call the "Already-Not Yet" tension of the old and new ages. Yet to look into your eyes each day is to feel the heat of the bush burning unconsumed, to glimpse the *eschaton*, to fall into the crevasse of the new world splitting from the old. I never knew that every inch of reality is sacred, until you appeared. My everyday miracles.

This is falling backwards, head-in-the-clouds love. Dostoevsky wrote, "The soul is healed by being with children."[3]

And then, just like Isaac, you enter the middle, and the children have become the teenagers. And it is different.

When they are young, parenting is a lot like running: it's about sweating and doing, just keeping up. You assume that for a period of years you will be tired and have no time to yourself. It's the trade you signed up for or you didn't sign up for, but it is what it is. At least you are largely in control of what's happening.

The middle has virtually none of this. You are not so needed for the basic routines of life and socialization. Some days it seems that you are not so needed at all. Navigating diapers and naps becomes navigating dating and driving. And those God-forsaken cell phones. One cultural critic described teenagers like this:

3. Crane, *Man is a Mystery*, 29.

> The world is passing through troublous times. The young
> people of today think of nothing but themselves. They
> have no reverence for parents or old age. They are impa-
> tient of all restraint. They talk as if they knew everything,
> and what passes for wisdom with us is foolishness with
> them. As for the girls, they are forward, immodest and
> unladylike in speech, behavior and dress.[4]

That critic's name was Peter the Hermit, and he lived a millennium ago. The tyranny of adolescence has been around for a
long time.

Some parents want the high of the downhill with no uphill
climb. They want to maintain the semblance of control they once
had, want their children to stay innocent forever. This is sad and
harmful, infantilizing. I've found that to embrace the uphill leads
to more downhills, more high. Parenting teenagers is different.
And it is good. And this is good.

Philo of Alexandria wrote: "For parents are midway between
the natures of God and man, and partake of both."[5] Parenting in
the middle, you get to feel both the human and the divine, to run
both sides of the mountain.

This is the end of that letter I wrote:

> Your originality is the full circle. It is the image of God
> within you. Let His image not be snuffed out. These days,
> looking at you, it is all that I can see.
>
> I leave you with a sentence I read from the Pulitzer prize
> winning novel, *Gilead*, in which a dying Congregational-
> ist minister reflects on the wonder of his child. "It's your
> existence I love you for, mainly."[6]

There are days when this is all that I know how to feel, what
to say.

4. Booker, *The Neophilacs*, 53.
5. Philo, *Volume 7*, 447.
6. Robinson, *Gilead*, 52.

19

Restarting: Generativity vs. Stagnation

Abraham took another wife, whose name was Keturah. She bore him Zimran, Jokshan, Medan, Midian, Ishbak and Shuah.—Genesis 25:1–2

Old men ought to be explorers
Here and there does not matter
We must be still and still moving
Into another intensity
For another union, a deeper communion

—T.S. Eliot, "East Coker"

THAT NIGHT WHEN I was running from the cannibals through the woods of middle Georgia, my choices were narrowing with every passing mile. I had already climbed the deer stand, trying to get my bearings. I simply had no clue, no compass. I listened for any sound of human activity: road noise, doors. Even if such sounds were present, the cicadas drowned everything out. My GPS watch, too primitive to have an actual map, just told me I was ten miles into the run. Suddenly, I thought I heard water.

The problem was that the sound I thought I heard did not align with the trail system. The trails were going back and forth, this sound was emanating from the side. I found a clearing under some powerlines which was a welcome sight in that electricity must lead to civilization. I took off down a long hill with weeds up to my chest, the clearing allowing the moon to light the way. I reached my destination and freeze. This was my definitive way out, but not at all the one I wanted.

The Ocmulgee River is 200 miles long, covering thirty-three counties in Georgia. In size it is rivaled only by the Chattahoochee in our state. There is a national monument erected to the history here, earthen mounds and pottery shards stretching back thousands of years. It still feeds some of the largest power plants in the south today. The name is Native American, one translation of which is "boiling water." This was not a creek.

What was worse, the local news had been reporting that the warming trend now had alligators up and down this stretch of the Ocmulgee. Parents who grew up fishing and swimming in it now told their children to stay away. I had a choice. I could play it safe or I could take the risk. Only one of those choices could bring me home.

It is not until the end of his life that the floodgates open. This is unnecessary, like grace.

Abraham has fulfilled the plan. Isaac has been born, blessed and married. The promise of the coming nation that will bless the earth is underway. After all that he has been through, all those miles traversed, all the heartbreak and joy, one would think this is enough. Time to retire. He can sit back and watch Isaac fall in love with his new wife. He can breathe deep of such hard-fought success. He is at peace with himself, even perhaps at peace, at long last, with God.

But he won't just hang it up. In Isaac, he has finally tasted of what is possible, of what eluded him for a century. If he doesn't have to wait anymore for such ecstasy, he won't. He can't. All of that walking, that living in between, has left him another chance that he could not have anticipated. So he gets right to it. I read this in a textbook on human development: "Generative adults commit themselves to the continuation and improvement of society as a whole through their connection to the next generation."[1] I don't know if this is exactly what Abraham had in mind, but I wouldn't put it past the old soldier.

Old Father Abraham marries again. Kids aren't ever taught this part of the story in Sunday School, but it's true. And even though he sure ought to be impotent at this stage of his life, now the joke is on Keturah. The first promise started with a laugh, and now the hilarity comes full circle. He ought to be in the geriatric ward himself, but instead Abraham is filling up the maternity ward. He's on a first-name basis with all of the nurses.

God promised young Abram that his lineage would one day become a great nation. Little could Abram have known this was a trick card. The next verses detail a multitude of nations that stemmed from Abraham's loins. Little wonder that Frederick Buechner starts his magisterial book on the gospel of Jesus with Abraham, a story, he says, that is "too good not to be true."[2] This deluge of extra sons, spinning off nations, legacies, l'embarras des richesses.

In 1968, Erik Erikson spun a theory about the middle of life, arguing that in middle age, the true struggle is between generativity and stagnation. Generativity might be achieved through professional achievements, guiding the young, or acts of cultural or artistic creation. His alternative definition for stagnation was self-absorption, which says it all. This is the fight in the middle, and it is a fight for your very life. It is a fight every day.

The lure of stagnation is typically based on some sense of having arrived. You have achieved some things, gained some stability. Like Abraham, you could just move into your waning years enjoying the Isaac you have made. Or you could reup and shoot for the moon. You could take a risk. You could generate.

There are so many stories of people reloading in the middle when they could have stagnated. My favorite is about the great orator and activist, perhaps the most well-known man in the world in the nineteenth century, Frederick Douglass.

1. Santrock, *Life-Span Development*, 499.
2. Buechner, *Telling the Truth*, 71.

In 1852, it appeared by all reasonable intents and purposes that the movement to abolish slavery in our country was going to fail. Things that seem inevitable on this side of history certainly were not, and for centuries the global economy depended on this institution, so it was not about to die quietly. The most famous ambassador of abolition was Douglass, the fugitive slave whose origins were so obscure he did not even know the year of his birth. Yet, in a time when oratory was a stadium sport, he was the G.O.A.T. He packed auditoriums across the US and Europe. He could hold a crowd in the palm of his hand and move them like no one else. But in 1852, after escaping slavery as a young man, then barnstorming the world for a decade, it looked like the cause of abolition was dead in the water.

Douglass would sometimes talk about a particular moment during this death spiral, another speech to a packed crowd, this time at the famed Faneuil Hall in Boston, where he had reached the end of his rope. He was exhausted, he was disheveled, he felt dismal and it showed. The great orator was stumbling over his words, his shoulders slouched, muddling his way through the speech with his eyes staring into space. He was going through the motions. He was spent and defeated.

But history turns on the smallest happenings, providence, and Sojourner Truth happened to be in the audience that day. I love that name. In the handful of pictures we have of her, you could imagine when that tiny woman entered the room, the ground shook. Like Douglass, she was born into slavery, escaped, and spent her whole life fighting for the cause. She changed her name to Sojourner Truth because she said God told her to, and I bet nobody argued with her about it.

Douglass was on the verge of collapse, but Truth (dear heaven) was in the audience that day. And after watching him practically bowled over the lectern, she could take it no more. In the middle of his speech, as it seemed to grind to a halt, she cried out, "Frederick, is God dead?"

For the rest of his life, he would point to that moment as a turning point, a catalyst, a shot across the bow. He went on to advise presidents, publish some of the world's best-selling books, and move the masses with his words for another half-century.

We need these experiences in the middle, after we have reared Isaac, and made our name great, and checked all the boxes. Freud was always dead wrong: what humanity needs is not pleasure or comfort or security. We need to be set on fire. All else is stagnation, which is just a nicer term for nihilism.

In my forties, I applied to be an officer in the United States Air Force Reserve Unit. It was half-witted and crazy. By the book, I am too old, so they had to request a special age waiver via several links up the chain of command. I would have to leave my family and my responsibilities to go to training camp for thirteen weeks where I would march and run and sleep in a cot beside recruits who are legitimately young enough to be my children. I was as certain that I could do it as I was as certain that I was scared to death. This was the lesson. I must generate, I must do this.

In a 1907 article in *Science Magazine* called "The Energies of Men," Harvard psychologist William James lamented the lost potential of our species, petrifying or just leaking away. "Compared with what we ought to be," he observed, "we are only half awake. Our fires are dampened, our drafts are checked. We are making use of only a small part of our possible mental and physical resources." Yes, we have limits, but they can technically be pushed beyond our imagination. As Abraham Maslow put it, "What a man can be, he must be."[3] Otherwise, what?

If you are in the middle, there is a Keturah somewhere in your hemisphere, there is an engine of generativity just waiting for you to kickstart. Perhaps like Abraham you have raised your kids but there are more out there somewhere. Maybe you need to sell the farm or buy one. Maybe you are discouraged but the real call is to redouble on what you're doing. Maybe you need to enlist in something greater than yourself. If any of this sounds nuts, I ask you, is God dead?

---

3. Maslow, *Motivation and Personality*, 46.

The other great first century rabbi, Hillel, described the middle part of his life so long ago: "I get up. I walk. I fall down. Meanwhile, I keep dancing."

20

Death: Training with the Gladiators

> Then Abraham breathed his last and died at a good old age, an old man and full of years; and he was gathered to his people.—Genesis 25:8

> "Because I am afraid of things, of being hurt, and death, I have to attempt them."—Terence Hanbury White

IT IS A TRUISM among athletes who are not connected to distance running that, one day, the clock runs out. Joints, endurance and mental acuity will, one day, give way. You will have to give up running and get a bicycle instead, the saying goes, and eventually you'll have to give that up too. We are, all of us, renting time, and one day the lease will be up.

But it's not true. The internet is littered with people qualifying for and finishing the world's top marathons in their eighties and nineties. They are women and men from all over the world. Gladys Burril ran the Honolulu Marathon at ninety-two, Jonathan Mendes the New York contest at ninety-six. Dimitrion Yordinidis ran the original marathon in Greece at ninety-eight, with a respectable time, too. Fauja Singh ran the Hong Kong 10k at 102. I read a piece from one runner that he made the painful decision to give up running ultramarathons in his seventies so he would be in better shape to run regular marathons in his eighties (are you kidding me?). Orville Rogers broke five world records at a hundred years old and routinely beats runners a generation younger in competition. He told the news media, "I live life with a capital L." I bet.

It seems outlandish because we are so blind and ignorant. It's not outlandish. It's just possible, like a lot of things. Sure, at my age I have about a zero percent chance of becoming an astronaut, or a sports broadcaster, or a drug lord. But I like to think that what will eventually stop my running is death alone, and when we meet, I hope they find my body on some trail somewhere, alone, with a smile on my face.

And so, we reach the end. It has been a journey of 175 years. We have no details surrounding his death, but how wonderful that Ishmael, the son of Abraham's faithlessness, buries his father alongside Isaac, the son of promise. And how odd that "after Abraham's death, God blessed his son Isaac," but not Ishmael (25:11). The story is an erratic, Siamese contradiction to the very end, a vast coupling of polarities. Brueggemann puts it starkly: "Ishmael is an unexpected way to conclude the Abraham story!"[1]

Though it seems pedestrian to ask about the meaning of Abraham at the end of this book, I suppose that sums it up. He is the first Jew, the progenitor of that people who would reshape the world. Majestically, they are the promise, and so the story invests them with the responsibility to live as promised people, a channel of divine blessing for the nations. But, as we have seen, most of this narrative is not at all that high-minded. Most of it is stumbling and grasping. Most of it is the gaps. The story of Abraham is more or less what any of us can expect out of life.

God is at the center of the story, of course, but this is no great comfort to many. Most of the time it isn't even a comfort to Abraham. In the narrative, God reminds me of Odysseus's long trek home, when he stops by to see Aeolus, the keeper of the winds. Aeolus gives him the winds in a bag for the rest of his journey, but when Odysseus tries to use them to aid the ship, chaos ensues, a tempest that they never figure out how to harness. Abraham never harnesses God, and God never really harnesses Abraham either.

1. Brueggemann, *Genesis*, 203.

"The expositor must take care not to explain," Brueggemann writes, "for it will not be explained. But without explanation, the text leads us to face the reality that God is God."[2]

If you are agnostic, you will chafe at Abraham's experience as any sort of life template (particularly the whole mock sacrifice of Isaac). If you are a person of faith, you want your beliefs to be much tidier, which is why Christians have been glossing this story forever, coming up with fancy interpretations about how the text doesn't really mean what it says, because God acts within our predictable schemas. I love that Jesus didn't do this, and neither did his Jewish tradition. This is why I have attempted to read the story with the ancient rabbis instead of other voices. They are the ones who truly embrace the messiness of Abraham.

Also, the story is about a good death, the death of a man who never stopped running.

Medieval Jews believed in 903 different kinds of death and said the best was death by "divine kiss," and Abraham was the first to have his soul kissed away. The Talmud says that his body has never decomposed.

Having procured all of the necessary waivers and having a mountain of paperwork approved over a 4-month process, I was finally ready to be medically cleared for military service. I was to arrive at what they call MEPS—Military Entrance Processing Station—south of Atlanta. My enlistment officer gave me specific instructions: be there at 4:45 AM, they will search your car, then line up at the glass door before the bus arrives with the requisite herd of teenagers. I did as I was told, and one eager young man had beaten me there. In our chat, I learned that he was seventeen years old, married with a child. God bless the South.

The physical was intense, about six hours of myriad exams, and I was a complete spectacle, the center of attention. They assumed I was a doctor or a lawyer and put me at the front of every line. At one point, I found myself stripped down to my underwear in a room with a bunch of teenagers, duckwalking

2. Brueggemann, *Genesis*, 188–189.

and squatting and running around the room, being shouted at and analyzed. I was just trying not to crack up. It was like I was enlisting in a high school summer camp as a camper, even as all of the officers called me "sir."

The final exam was one-on-one with an Army physician, going over your whole body. I passed every test until the end. "There's one thing I want you to get checked out. It's probably nothing. Send us the report and we'll clear you."

A few weeks later, another doctor said, "You have cancer." Two days after that, I had surgery for the first time in my life. Just before I went under, the surgeon said, "That army doctor probably saved your life." He paused for a while in the middle of that sentence.

When you are a child, there is an expanse when time has no meaning to you, and then a moment that time starts. Toward the middle, there is an expanse when death has no meaning to you, and then a moment that it does. At thirty, death never crossed my mind. But in the middle, diagnoses can happen. There are dark spots of depression, moments of wanting to take to the road and never come back. There are questions about the impact of your life, now that you have made it here. Life is not all futurity anymore, it is panoramic, which can be a disorienting vantage point. At some point, you come to realize that you don't have forever. A piece of graffiti uncovered in the ruins of ancient Pompeii simply reads, "While I am alive, you, hateful death, are coming."

Maybe that is why I run.

There is an ancient graveyard in Turkey that was recently discovered, and it was a specific burial site for famous Roman gladiators. The skeletons of sixty-seven gladiators have been examined by scientists, corroborating the evidence from literary sources about the rigor of their training. The bulk of the evidence proves that these gladiators were sequestered from society, fed a lavish diet, and enjoyed expensive medical treatment. They were heroes, idols, overpaid athletes.

The games that they prepared for were little more than grotesque public stunts. Exotic beast hunts, sickeningly creative executions, and staged combat scenes involving hundreds of fighters were constructed to appeal to public bloodlust. The fact that the spectacles also included free food for the public caused the first-century poet, Juvenal, to famously lament: "The people that once bestowed commands, consulships, legions, and all else, now concerns itself no more, and longs eagerly for just two things—bread and circuses." Kind of like professional glam wrestling, the WWE, the gladiators weren't actually the ones killed in the arenas. That was reserved for the prisoners, and sometimes the Christians.

We don't know exactly when it started, but about the time the New Testament writings were complete, a Roman governor wrote a letter to Emperor Trajan which survives, asking for counsel on how to deal with these miscreant Christians. The governor, named Pliny, had killed some because he figured it was a good precedent ("For I do not doubt that, whatever the character of the crime may be which they confess, their pertinacity and inflexible obstinacy certainly ought to be punished."[3]), but wanted imperial approval. A century later, killing Christians in the games was something of a cottage entertainment industry. And there were enough Christians who weren't afraid to die that certain bishops tried to calm them down, as a Christian "cult of the martyrs" fueled this fascination with death in the arenas. But that is not my point.

Emerging scholarship is finding remarkable parallels between the training periods of ancient gladiators and early Christians preparing for martyrdom. Both were major actors in the arena spectacles. Both were carefully selected by their communities. Both were fed a special diet. Both received the *sacramentum*, or sacred meal, the night before the spectacle. It appears that early Christian martyrs mimicked the training of the gladiators who would gruesomely kill them. They had to train harder than the gladiators because their subversive plan was to beat their Roman executioners at their own game. They refused to be the butt of spectacle. They wanted to subvert it and die like a hero.

3. Pliny, *The Letters of Pliny the Younger: Book VI-X*, 270.

"Do not go gentle into that good night," wrote the poet Dylan Thomas.

> Old age should burn and rave at close of day;
> Rage, rage against the dying of the light.[4]

I'm convinced that we don't make this decision at the end. We make it in the middle, the decision of whether to capitalize the L in our life. We can run, train for death even as we rage against it. Or we can settle, stagnate, fade away.

As for me, I'll be running.

---

4. Thomas, *The Poems of Dylan Thomas*, 239.

Epilogue

I EMERGED FROM THE torrent of the Ocmulgee River, heart racing, having swam like Michael Phelps. It turns out that the thought of complete disappearance without a trace is quite the motivator. I climbed up a steep, muddy bank, fell on my back. I climbed up again to encounter a thorn thicket. It took half an hour to make my way through, inch by inch, bleeding from head to ankles. I found a road and thought about flagging down a truck, but this is middle Georgia, where everyone has a gun under their seat, and I look like I have certainly been involved in a crime. I keep running and find my way home, having developed a fever from the physical toll of it all, this hobo duathlon.

That was the turning point, like a baptism, like Abraham moving off the map. The Ocmulgee experience demarcated my young life from the middle.

When I turned forty, an odd thing happened. I hadn't even really aspired to it. I had been running hard races for so long that you are just glad to finish respectably, perhaps in the top 10-20 percent. That alone is like breaking a hundred in golf; very few will ever do it. Heck, only half a percent of the American population ever even try to start a 5k one time in their lives.

Then, out of nowhere, I made it to the podium in a two-hour trail race. Then, in the next one, I made it again. Then, I won. And like Forrest Gump, I just kept it up. Roger Bannister, the first to break the four-minute mile when most thought it impossible, described the shift. "To move into the lead means making an act requiring fierceness and confidence," he said. "But fear must play some part . . . no relaxation is possible, and all discretion is thrown to the wind."[1] There is a headiness to winning.

To be sure, most of the time I was winning my newly achieved age bracket, where the competition isn't so stiff. But the thrill of having your name called and standing on the box, looking down at everyone else, never goes away. I believe this is the joy of the middle.

If you have kept your nose clean and not fallen apart, neither of which are small feats, you get to enjoy it. You get to breathe. You get to calm the voice of fear and talk back to the voice of inadequacy. You can't do this at twenty-one because you haven't won anything. The middle is a place of tumult but can also be a place of rest.

It seems like this was Abraham's experience in the middle, especially when he named the promised son Laughter. He finally made it to the podium.

In 1962, a young Air Force corporal named Dick Hoyt was thrilled to welcome his new son into the world. Like many new fathers, he was filled with hope about what his son might achieve and who his son might become. Those hopes were dashed, however, when his son was diagnosed as a spastic quadriplegic with cerebral palsy. He would never walk, never talk, and there was no hope.

Except in this new father's heart, hope wouldn't die. Instead, he threw himself into the life of his son, refusing to keep him away from normal boyhood activities. Although the son was virtually paralyzed, he took him swimming and sledding, pushed the public school system to include his son, and taught him to read. When he was 10 years old, this father scored a partnership with leading engineers at Tufts University, who developed a computer that the speechless son would be able to use to communicate. His first

1. McDougall, *Born to Run*, 84.

words with that computer weren't, "Hi mom," but "Go Bruins!" The kid was a sports fan to the core.

When he was fifteen years old, he told his dad through this computer that he wanted to run in a local charity 5K race. His dad was no runner but said he would give it a shot, so he pushed his son in his wheelchair all 3.2 miles, finishing in second to last place. That night, his son told him, "Dad, when I'm running, I don't feel handicapped."

Ever since that day, this father-son team has been on a journey that has captured the hearts of millions. They have run, swam, and biked hundreds of marathons, duathlons, triathlons, and even six of the toughest races on earth—the Ironman—together, with the father pulling or pushing his son the entire way. In 1992, they ran and biked across the United States, 3,735 miles, in just 45 days. And even though one man is doing all the running, they call themselves, "Team Hoyt."

What I have come to realize in the middle, is that all of this time, it has not been me doing all the running.

In Genesis, Abraham never blesses his son, Isaac. Instead, "after Abraham's death, God blessed his son Isaac" (25:11). Abraham, the patriarch, faithless and faithful, and YHWH, the faithful One.

Bibliography

Barber, Andrea. Full Circle. New York: Citadel, 2019.

Berry, Wendell. The Selected Poems of Wendell Berry. Berkeley: Counterpoint, 1998.

Bessey, Sarah. Miracles and Other Reasonable Things. A Story of Unlearning and Relearning God. New York: Howard, 2019.

Booker, Christopher. The Neophiliacs. London: Pimlico, 1992.

Brand, Paul and Philip Yancey. The Gift of Pain: Why We Hurt and what We Can Do about it. Grand Rapids: Zondervan, 1997.

Brooks, David. The Second Mountain: The Quest for a Moral Life. New York: Random House, 2019.

Brueggemann, Walter. "The Costly Loss of Lament." In The Psalms: The Life of Faith, edited by Patrick D. Miller, 98–111. Minneapolis: Fortress, 1995.

———. "Counterscript." The Christian Century, November 29, 2005.

———. Genesis. Louisville: Westminster John Knox, 1982.

Buber, Martin. Daniel: Dialogues on Realization. Austin, TX: Holt, Rinehart and Winston, 1964.

———. I and Thou. Translated by Walter Kaufman. New York: Simon & Schuster, 1970.

———. Tales of the Hasidim. Translated by Olga Marx. New York: Schocken, 1947.

Buechner, Frederick. Beyond Words: Daily Readings in the ABC's of Faith. New York: Harper, 2004.

———. On the Road with the Archangel. New York: Harper, 1997.

———. Telling the Truth: The Gospel as Tragedy, Comedy and Fairy Tale. New York: Harper, 1977.

———. The Remarkable Ordinary: How to Stop, Look, and Listen to Life. Grand Rapids: Zondervan, 2017.

Calvin, John. Institutes of the Christian Religion. Translated by Elsie Anne McKee. Grand Rapids: Eerdmans, 2009.

Chappell, Sophia Grace. Epiphanies: An Ethics of Experience. Oxford: Oxford University Press, 2022.

Cox Media Group, "Neil deGrasse Tyson Believes we could be Living in Matrix-like Simulation." April 25, 2016. Accessed March 1, 2023. https://www.daytondailynews.com/news/national/neil-degrasse-tyson-believes-could-living-matrix-like-simulation/vFcXrFS2SZt4wB6A1cWOFM/

Crane, Bruce. Man is a Mystery: a Collection of Dostoyevsky's Thoughts on the Human Condition. New York: Writers Club, 2001.

Crosby, Cindy, ed. Ancient Christian Devotional. Downers Grove, IL: InterVarsity, 2007.

Curry, Thomas W. "With Head Held High: Preaching Hope in a Noisy Time." Journal for Preachers 42 (2018) 2–7.

Davis, William Stearns. A Day in Old Athens: A Picture of Athenian Life. New York: Allyn & Bacon, 1914.

Dederer, Claire. Monsters: A Fan's Dilemma. New York: Alfred A. Knopf, 2023.

Delaney, Matt. "Jim Redmond, Who Helped Injured Son Limp across Finish Line in 1922 Olympics, Dies at 81." Washington Times, October 4, 2022.

Dillard, Annie. Pilgrim at Tinker Creek. New York: Harper's, 1974.

———. Teaching a Stone to Talk: Expeditions and Encounters. New York: Harper Perennial, 1982.

Dostoevsky, Fylodor. The Brothers Karamazov. Translated by Richard Pevear and Larissa Volokhonsky. New York: Farrar, Straus and Giroux, 1990.

Eliot, T.S. The Complete Poems and Plays: 1909-1950. New York: Harcourt Brace & Company, 1952.

Ellis, Nicholas J. "The Reception of the Jobraham Narratives in Jewish Thought." In |Authoritative Texts and Reception History, edited by Dan Batovici, et al., 124-140. Boston: Brill, 2017.

Emerson, Ralph Waldo. The Portable Emerson, edited by Jeffrey S. Cramer. New York: Penguin, 2014.

Endean, Philip. Karl Rahner and Ignatian Spirituality. Oxford: Oxford University Press, 2004.

Feiler, Bruce. Abraham: A Journey to the Heart of Three Faiths. New York: Perennial, 2004.

Francis, Enjoli and Eric Noll. "100-Year-Old Runner Sets 5 New US and World Track Records." March 19, 2018. Accessed January 7, 2023. https://abcnews.go.com/US/100-year-runner-sets-us-world-track-records/story?id=53859293

Frymer-Kensky, Tikva. "Akeda: A View from the Bible." In Beginning Anew: A Woman's Companion to the High Holy Days, edited by Gail Twersky Reimer et al., 127-44. New York: Touchstone, 1997.

Gathercole, Simon. The Gospel of Thomas: Introduction and Commentary. Boston: Brill, 2014.

Ginzberg, Louis. The Legends of the Jews. Translated by Henrietta Szold. Columbia, SC: Pantanios Classics, 1909.

Green, Emma. "Advice on Writing from The Atlantic's Ta-Nehisi Coates." The Atlantic, September 7, 2013.

Gregory of Nyssa. Saint Gregory of Nyssa Collection. Chicago: Aeterna, 2016.

Gruen, Arno. Betrayal of the Self: The Fear of Autonomy in Men and Women. New York: Grover, 1988.

Haldane, J.B.S. Possible Worlds and Other Essays. London: Chatto and Windus, 1927.

Harari, Yuval Noah. Sapiens: A Brief History of Humankind. New York: Harper Perennial, 2015.

Haxby, Mikael. "The Gladiator Graveyard of Ephesus as Evidence for the Study of Martyrdom." In The First Urban Churches 3: Ephesus, edited by James R. Harrison et al., 171–192. Atlanta: SBL, 2018.

Hayden, Christopher J., dir. 2002. Marathon Monks of Mount Hiei. Documentary Educational Resources.

Hedges, Christopher. Empire of Illusion: The End of Literacy and the Triumph of Spectacle. New York: Nation, 2009.

Hershon, Paul Isaac. A Talmudic Miscellany. Boston: Houghton, Mifflin and Co., 1880.

Heschel, Abraham Joshua. Heavenly Torah: As Refracted Through the Generations. New York: Continuum, 2006.

Heschel, Susannah. "What the March at Selma Means to the Jews." Pittsburgh Jewish Chronicle, January 21, 2015.

Hoyt, Dick. Devoted: The Story of a Father's Love For His Son. Cambridge: Da Capo, 2010.

Huysmans, J.K. Against the Grain. Translated by John Howard. New York: Albert & Charles Boni, 1924.

James, William. "The Energies of Men." Science (1907) 321–332.

Jung, Carl G. Man and His Symbols. London: Aldus, 1971.

Kalanithi, Paul. When Breath Becomes Air. New York: Random House, 2016.

Kass, Leon R. The Beginning of Wisdom: Reading Genesis. Chicago: University of Chicago Press, 2003.

Keh, Andrew. "Eliud Kipchoge Breaks Two-Hour Marathon Barrier." New York Times, October 12, 2019.

Kenyon, E.W. and Don Gossett. His Word is Now. New Kensington, PA: Whitaker House, 2016.

Kierkegaard, Soren. Fear and Trembling. Translated by Howard V. Hong and Edna H. Hong. Princeton: Princeton University Press, 1983.

———. For Self-Examination. Translated by Howard V. Hong and Edna H. Hong. Princeton: Princeton University Press, 1990.

Knight, Phil. Shoe Dog. New York: Scribner, 2016.

Kugel, James L. The Bible As It Was. Cambridge: Belknap, 1997.

Lamott, Anne. Bird by Bird: Some Instructions on Writing and Life. New York: Anchor, 1994.

————. Help, Thanks Wow: Three Essential Prayers. New York: Riverhead, 2012.

————. Traveling Mercies: Some Thoughts on Faith. New York: Pantheon, 1999.

Levinson, Daniel J. The Seasons of a Man's Life. New York: Ballantine Books, 1978.

Lewis, C.S. The C.S. Lewis Signature Classics. New York: Harper One, 2017.

Luscombe, Belinda. "Do we Need $75,000 a Year to be Happy?" Time, September 6, 2010.

MacDonald, Helen. H is for Hawk. New York: Grove, 2014.

MacGregor, Neil. A History of the World in 100 Objects. New York: Viking, 2011.

Maslow, Abraham. Motivation and Personality. New York: Harper & Row, 1981.

McDougall, Christopher. Born to Run: A Hidden Tribe, Superathletes, and the Greatest Race the World Has Never Seen. New York: Alfred A. Knoff, 2009.

Merton, Thomas. The Wisdom of the Desert: Sayings from the Desert Fathers of the Fourth Century. Boston: Shambhala, 2004.

Middleton, J. Richard. Abraham's Silence: The Binding of Isaac, the Suffering of Job, and How to Talk Back to God. Grand Rapids: Baker Academic, 2021.

Neusner, Jacob. The Mishnah: A New Translation. New Haven: Yale University Press, 1988.

Nouwen, Henri. Life of the Beloved: Spiritual Living in a Secular World. New York: Crossroad, 1992.

O'Connor, Flannery. Collected Works. New York: Literary Classics of the United States, 1988.

Painter, Nell Irvin. Sojourner Truth: A Life, A Symbol. New York: W.W. Norton, 1996.

Phipps, William E. Mark Twain's Religion. Macon, GA: Mercer University Press, 2003.

Pliny. The Letters of the Younger Pliny: Book VI-X. Translated by John Benjamin Firth. London: Walter Scott, 1900.

Reagon, Bernice Johnson. If You Don't Go, Don't Hinder Me: The African American Sacred Song Tradition. Lincoln, NE: University of Nebraska Press, 2001.

Renoir, Jean, dir. 1939. La règle du jeu. G.M. Films.

Rice, Anne. Christ the Lord: Out of Egypt. New York: Ballantine, 2006.

Rice, Joshua. "Apocalyptic Christmas." Journal for Preachers (2013) 33–38.

Rilke, Rainer Maria. Letters to a Young Poet. Translated by M.D. Herter. New York: Norton, 1934.

Robinson, Marilynne. Gilead. New York: Picador, 2006.

Rohr, Richard. The Universal Christ: How a Forgotten Reality can Change Everything we See, Hope for, and Believe. New York: Convergent, 2021.

Rumi, Mevlana Jalaluddin. The Rumi Collection, edited by Kabir Helminski. Boston: Shambhala, 2000.

Saldarani, Anthony J. "Rabbinic Literature and the NT." In Anchor Bible Dictionary 5:602–604.

Samuel, Michael Leo. Rediscovering Philo of Alexandria: A First Century Torah Commentator. Sarasota, FL: First Edition Design, 2016.

Santrock, John W. Life-Span Development. 18th ed. New York: McGraw Hill, 2021.

Sides, Hampton. In the Kingdom of Ice: The Grand and Terrible Polar Voyage of the USS Jeannette. New York: Doubleday, 2014.

Smith, Wes. "Knights of Chonda-Za." Chicago Tribune, December 19, 1988.

Soelle, Dorothee. The Silent Cry: Mysticism and Resistance. Translated by Barbara and Martin Rumscheidt. Minneapolis: Fortress, 2001.

Stevens, John. The Marathon Monks of Mount Hiei. Brattleboro, VT: Echo Point, 1988.

Suwaed, Muhammed. Historical Dictionary of the Bedouins. New York: Rowman & Littlefield, 2015.

Tennyson, Alfred. The Complete Poetical Works of Alfred, Lord Tennyson. New York: Harper & Brothers, 1884.

The Onion. "New Remote Control can be Operated by Remote." February 5, 1997. Accessed February 1, 2023. https://www.theonion.com/new-remote -control-can-be-operated-by-remote-1819564183.

Thomas, Dylan. The Poems of Dylan Thomas, Volume 1. New York: New Directions, 2003.

Tillich, Paul. The Shaking of the Foundations. New York: Charles Scribner's Sons, 1948.

Tolstoy, Leo. Anna Karenina. Cambridge: Cambridge University Press, 1987.

Tyerman, L. The Life and Times of the Rev. John Wesley. London: Hodder and Stoughton, 1870.

Tyson, Mike. Undisputed Truth. New York: Plume, 2013.

Vaillant, George E. Adaptation to Life. Cambridge: Harvard University Press, 1977.

Virgil. The Aeneid. Translated by J.W. Mackail. London: Collector's Library, 2004.

White, T.H. England Have My Bones. New York: Penguin, 1982.

Wiesel, Ellie. Sages and Dreamers: Biblical, Talmudic, and Hasidic Portraits and Legends. New York: Summit, 1991.

Winner, Lauren. Girl Meets God: On the Path to a Spiritual Life. Chapel Hill, NC: Algonquin, 2002.